OUR C

Our God Reigns

Reflections on the character of God

RAY McCAULEY

KINGSWAY PUBLICATIONS
EASTBOURNE

First published 1985 by Marshall Morgan and Scott Ltd

First British edition 1991

Front cover: Zefa Picture Library

British Library Cataloguing in Publication Data

McCauley, Ray
Our God reigns.
1. Christianity. Religious life
I. Title
248.4

ISBN 0–86065–939–9

Printed in Great Britain for
KINGSWAY PUBLICATIONS LTD
1 St Anne's Road, Eastbourne, E Sussex BN21 3UN by
BPCC Hazell Books, Aylesbury, Bucks
Typeset by Watermark, Crostwight, Norfolk

Contents

1
The character of God

1. Laying a foundation

One of the greatest blessings I ever had when I was in Tulsa at Bible School, was to find out the character of God. I remember that my wife, sitting next to me, wept when she really began to know Abba (Father). When we get to know God as *'Daddy'*, our whole understanding of the Word of God changes.

Unfortunately, many members of the Body of Christ today don't really know their Father. If they did, they wouldn't say the things they do about Him – God gets the blame for everything. We need to understand our relationship with our heavenly Father, which can be even closer than the relationship we have with our father here on earth. We should be able to sit down and say, 'Daddy, I want to ask you about this,' or, 'Dad, will you show me that?' or, 'What do you think about this, Dad?' Have you ever spoken to your Father in Heaven on the same basis that you speak to your father on this earth? Our Father God is even more understanding, He has more wisdom, and He is more loving than any earthly father could ever be! We need to see Him that way. We need to see that we can have fellowship with Him on that level. And we need to reach the point where we can see, through the Word of God, what type of character He has.

Many people have been married for fifty years and still

don't really know each other. You can be married all your life and never really know your wife. You can be a Christian all your life, and never know God the Father. I've heard people in the mission field say, 'You know, I'm so terrified that God will send me somewhere I really don't want to go.' Well, the Bible says, 'If you delight yourself in the Lord, he will give you the desires of your heart' (Ps. 37.4). He will give it to you – He puts the desire in your heart. When God calls you to do something, He will put the desire in your heart. He is not the author of confusion. God is hardly likely to send someone who is allergic to sand, to Egypt! God is not going to call someone to pastor a church when that person has absolutely no desire to be a pastor. Now someone might say, 'But, I know of a person who said that he never wanted to be a pastor but found himself pastoring a church.' If that man is a true pastor, then it was his head telling him not to be a pastor – not his heart. Most of the time we are led by our heads and not our hearts. But when we begin to follow our heart, we will find that it is more fun doing what God puts in our heart than listening to our head.

As you begin to study the character of God through His Word, you will discover that God is a *good God* – and He is not out there with a big stick, just waiting to get you! He is doing everything in His power to keep you alive, to get you born again and to bless you. God is not out there planning to destroy you.

We need to know the character of God: *Firstly*, because our faith begins where the will of God is known.

There is confusion in the Body of Christ today, where people do not know that God's will is His Word and His Word is His will. If you don't know that it is God's will to heal you, you can never have faith to believe God for your healing.

Secondly, because when you know what God's will is in a situation then you can fight the good fight of faith – you can apply the spiritual principles for God's will to be done in the situation.

And, *thirdly*, because then you can stand wearing the armour of God.

However, many people will go to God in ignorance concerning His will and say, 'God, you are in control whatever will be, will be,' and be unable to pray the prayer of faith. God gave us the Bible so we would know His will. His Word is His will. Now there may be a time in your life when you need to spend time before God to find out what your calling is – that would be a prayer of dedication and consecration. But most of the time we will find God's will for us in His Word.

Of course, there are some things we need to know which are not in His Word, such as 'Do I marry John Smith?' You would have to seek God in this area until there is a peace in your spirit regarding the answer. Also, God does not specifically say that you are called to Hawaii or to the Cape beaches – it might be somewhere else! Again, you need to seek God regarding your calling. But concerning blessings, health, prosperity, and spiritual life, He states His will for you in His Word. God wants us to have abundant life – we read that in John 10.10. We know that it is God's will to save us – we see it in His Word, and when we know it is God's will for us to be healed, we can apply our faith to it.

Now someone might ask, 'Well, if God is so willing to answer our prayers, why doesn't He answer them?' The problem is with the person and not with God, and he needs to study the Scriptures and spend time in prayer to find out why. God's Word says that if you abide in Him and His Word abides in you, you shall ask what you will and it shall be done unto you, that He may be glorified and that you may bear much fruit (John 15.7–8).

We need to understand that *God is on our side*. God wants your family to be saved – He wants you to live in perfect harmony – He wants you to walk in divine health, to be filled with His Holy Spirit and to speak in other tongues. God wants you to worship Him, to praise Him, to serve Him, and He wants you to walk in His perfect will twenty-four hours a day. The Bible begins to reveal His character to us.

2. Spending time in the Word of God

Many people have the idea that God is mysterious and that it is impossible really to understand the Word of God – that one can never fully comprehend what is in the Bible. Charles Capps said, 'The Bible is so simple that you have to find someone to help you misunderstand it!' We need to get back to the Word of God and not to what people think about the Word.

> The secret things belong unto the Lord our God: but those things which are revealed belong unto us and to our children forever, that we may do all the words of this law (Deut. 29.29).

Everything that is written in the Word of God belongs to us. If God says that the secret things belong to Him then He will not have written down those secret things – a secret is something you keep to yourself. You don't write out a secret and publish it in a book. So the Word of God has been revealed to us and we have the Holy Spirit to teach us.

God has placed in the ministry, apostles, prophets, evangelists, pastors and teachers but it is the Holy Spirit who teaches the Body of Christ through those men. It is the Holy Spirit who individually teaches every member of the Body. As we begin to meditate on the Word, we receive more and more revelation.

Some people have said, 'God moves in a mysterious way His wonders to perform, so don't expect to understand what is going on.' But God has revealed so much to us in His Word – we have to play our part and meditate on that Word, and then He will begin to teach us more and more.

If we will spend time with God in His Word, He will answer questions for us in our personal life. He will show us where we have missed it, why we are sick, why there is a problem in a certain area. God does not reveal things to us when it is really none of our business. For instance, someone says, 'I want to know why Mrs Smith died.' Well, that is between Mrs Smith and Jesus, and no one else. But God will speak to us regarding our own personal lives through His Word.

The Word of God has been revealed to us and it is our responsibility to understand it – it is not a mysterious book. Before we are born again, it is like reading *Disney World* – impossible to understand. But once we are born again, if we spend time with God and pray in the Spirit while we read the Bible, God will reveal the knowledge of His Word.

> Thus saith the Lord, Let not the wise man glory in his wisdom, neither let the mighty man glory in his might, let not the rich man glory in his riches: But let him that glorieth glory in this, that he understandeth and knoweth me, that I am the Lord which exercise loving kindness, judgment, and righteousness, in the earth: for in these things I delight, saith the Lord (Jer. 9.23–24).

We need to understand and know God.

No earthly father who loves his son, would deliberately injure him or make him sick, even if he had disobeyed him, or misbehaved. The father would be hurt; he would probably let the son know he was disappointed but he wouldn't want to break his arm or leg or put him in hospital for a month. How then can we accuse our loving Heavenly Father God of doing these things to His children? How can we accuse Him of making us sick to teach us something? We need to know that our Father God loves us even more than any earthly father. As we look at a loving father son relationship in the natural world, we will begin to see our Heavenly Father more clearly.

> If a son shall ask bread of any of you that is a father, will he give him a stone? or if he ask a fish, will he for a fish give him a ser-

pent? Or if he shall ask an egg, will he offer him a scorpion? If ye then, being evil, know how to give good gifts unto your children: how much more shall your heavenly Father give the Holy Spirit to them that ask him? (Luke 11.11–13).

The Lord is gracious, and full of compassion; slow to anger and of great mercy. The Lord is good to all; and his tender mercies are over all his works (Ps. 145.8–9).

3. God tempts no man

The Bible tells us that Christians will be confronted with tests and trials:

Blessed is the man that endureth temptation: for when he is tried, he shall receive the crown of life, which the Lord hath promised to them that love him. Let no man say when he is tempted, I am tempted of God: for God cannot be tempted with evil, neither tempteth he any man (Jas. 1.12–13).

James tells us that God cannot tempt any man with evil, but He will test your faith, because if He does not, we cannot exercise faith and, therefore, we cannot grow. We will have to exercise our own faith to get out of a situation. It is not God's purpose to perform a miracle every two minutes for us – His purpose is for us to stand on the Word, exercise our faith, and walk out of that situation. How we react is what will determine how strong our faith is. *But God will never test us with evil, never tempt us with evil, He will never try us with evil.*

Jesus said, 'The thief cometh not, but for to steal, and to kill, and to destroy: I am come that they might have life, and that they might have it more abundantly' (John 10.10).

If anything has been stolen from us, it is *not* God teaching us something – God is not taking the lives of little children – God is *not* destroying. We, indirectly, might be causing trouble to come upon ourselves through disobedience to God's Word. The conditions attached to the Bible promises are there in order to protect us from the evil one. When we understand this truth, we can understand why we need to obey the Word of God.

Someone says, 'Well, I don't know why this is happening to me. I just don't know why my prayers are not being answered.' Yet that person has not been speaking to his wife for a week! The Bible says that if we walk in strife, we are taken captive of the devil at his will; that when we stand praying, we must forgive if we have ought against any, that our Father may forgive us; that faith worketh by love. God's conditions are not in His Word simply to spoil our fun! They are there for our protection.

Life gets better and better when I live according to the Word of God. Someone once asked, 'Does it mean that I have to give up smoking?' No, it doesn't, but you might just have to exercise strong faith against cancer in a few years' time! Someone asked, 'If you smoke, can you go to heaven?' Yes, and you might get there much quicker too!

> But every man is tempted, when he is drawn away of his own lust, and enticed. Then when lust hath conceived, it bringeth forth sin: and sin, when it is finished, bringeth forth death (Jas. 1.14–15).

Some people think God hates sin because He doesn't like people having a good time. No, He hates sin because sin will kill you. Some of the most powerful, influential and famous people in the world have died in poverty and unhappiness – not financial poverty but spiritual poverty. Sin has destroyed them.

> Do not err, my beloved brethren. Every good gift and every perfect gift is from above, and cometh down from the Father of lights, with whom is no variableness, neither shadow of turning (Jas. 1.16–17).

The Lord showed me that this means that He gives every

good and perfect gift, and He will never change from giving good and perfect gifts; that He is the same yesterday, today and for ever; that He will always be the Father of lights and He will always give us good and perfect gifts.

Someone may say, 'Why is God allowing so many things to happen to me?' In the Old Testament, we read:

> I call heaven and earth to record this day against you, that I have set before you life and death, blessing and cursing: therefore choose life, that both thou and thy seed may live (Deut. 30.19).

That is not only for you, but for your family as well. *The choice is yours.*

There is enough sickness, poverty and death for everybody in this world. The curse is still in existence. But God has sent His only begotten Son who became the firstborn from the dead – He went to the cross and shed His blood so that we could have eternal life. When we choose to take Jesus as our Lord, then we are redeemed from the curse (Gal. 3.13). The Bible says that God will not see the righteous forsaken or begging bread (Ps. 37.25).

We need to know the Word of God. We need to confess what God says about us in His Word – what He has provided for us in His Word. We need to know that He has made us righteous (2 Cor. 5.21).

For too long we have been deceived by the devil, and now the Body of Christ is beginning to see who the enemy is, who the Father is, and who they are in Christ. It is time we started redeeming those things that belong to us. We cannot be a blessing unless we are blessed.

4. Serving God because we love Him

God says He will supply all our need according to His riches in glory by Christ Jesus (Phil. 4.19). If God says it, I believe it, and it will come to pass. That is the relationship we need to have with our Father God.

We are told in the New Testament that we have a better covenant than in the Old Testament – established on better promises:

> But now hath he obtained a more excellent ministry, by how much also he is the mediator of a better covenant, which was established upon better promises. But without faith it is impossible to please him; for he that cometh to God must believe that he is, and that he is a rewarder of them that diligently seek him (Heb. 8.6 and Heb. 11.6).

He is not a taker, but a rewarder. He will give us everything we need when we diligently seek Him:

> But seek ye first the Kingdom of God, and his righteousness; and all these things shall be added unto you (Matt. 6.33).

Many of the Jews could not tolerate the teachings of Jesus because they could not understand the character of God. When Jesus said, 'If you've seen me, you've seen the Father,' they could not understand that God could have a character like Jesus. They didn't know God as their Father.

> No man can come to me, except the Father which hath sent me draw him: and I will raise him up at the last day. It is written in the prophets. And they shall be all taught of God. Every man therefore that hath heard, and hath learned of the Father, cometh unto me (John 6.44–45).

As you get to know the character of God, you begin to love Jesus so much more.

Let me share this illustration with you:

A father has two sons. He comes home one day and says to the first son, 'John, I want you to go out and mow the lawn.'

He says, 'Dad, do I have to do that?'

'Yes, John, if you don't go out and mow the lawn you're

going to get a hiding. And when I come back in two hours' time and that lawn is not mowed, I'm going to take away your allowance, I'm going to lock you in a room and I'm going to give you the hiding of your life.'

John starts mowing the lawn, muttering to himself, 'My cruel father, making me mow the lawn all day. He's such a terrible person.' And he gets more and more resentful.

The father comes home the next day and says to the second son, 'Now, Simon, will you do me a favour?'

'Sure, Dad, anything you want me to do, it's a privilege just to do anything for you.'

The father says, 'Okay, son, will you mow the lawn?'

'Dad that's great, I'll do it any time you ever ask me to do it.'

Simon starts mowing the lawn and thinks, 'Gee, what a privilege it is to do this for my Dad.'

The second son's relationship and fellowship with his Dad will stay constant for the rest of their lives. The first son is going to have a backsliding situation with his father almost immediately.

When we love Jesus, we desire only to do what He wants us to do; the Spirit of God changes us. People do not have to be told what they have to give up in order to come to Jesus. When they receive Jesus as Lord, they will give those things up anyway. But when people are told that unless they receive Jesus, they may be struck by lightning or run over by a car, and go to hell, their commitment to God will not last. They will be serving God through fear and not love.

Many people in the Body of Christ have been taught to be afraid of God and so they serve Him reluctantly through fear. They never get to know the love of God. Consequently, it is not a surprise when that person begins to backslide. It is only when people begin to realise how much God loves them and how rewarding it is to serve Jesus, that they can begin to walk in fellowship with God.

5. God dwelling in us

People in the world have many different views of God. Some believe He is a universal 'something' floating about in the atmosphere. Some think He is impersonal, immaterial and intangible. Some believe He is a universal mind, or an abstract power or force filling the universe. But the truth is that God is a spirit being, and as we have seen, He is our Father – our Daddy. Jesus called Him 'Abba' or 'Father' and we are His children so we can call Him 'Abba' or 'Father' too.

God actually comes to dwell in us when we are born again. Paul said in Acts 17.28, 'For in him we live and move, and have our being.' We need to get the full revelation of that verse. Many people say, 'I can't go in there and minister to that person – I won't know what to say.' But if God lives in us, we can! The Holy Spirit will lead and guide us.

We need to realise that *God lives in us* if we are born again children of God.

> Jesus answered and said unto him, If a man love me, he will keep my words; and my Father will love him, and we will come unto him, and make our abode with him (John 14.23).

Only when a person makes their home with someone and lives with them, do they develop an intimate personal relationship. God has actually come to live with us so that we can have a close intimate relationship with Him.

6. The redemptive names of God

Jesus prayed to God: 'And this is life eternal, that they might know thee, the only true God' (John 17.3). God's desire is for you to know Him as He is. There is no reasonable excuse for ignorance of God, for there are over 20,000 references to Him in the Word stating in detail what He is like, what He can do, what He has done, and what He plans to do. His names are found over 1,900 times in the Scriptures.

Many people who believe in God do not know His names through which He reveals Himself and so they have the wrong image of God. If I said, 'Dog' to you, you would not have a clear picture of the dog. But if I said, 'Big dog' you would have a little bit more information. If I said, 'Big, black dog' . . . 'Big, black, bad tempered dog' . . . 'Big, black, bad tempered, vicious, Alsatian dog', you would then have a very good image of the dog.

So the more names God has in the Word, the more His character is revealed. When He spoke to the Israelites, the names he gave them meant something. For instance, 'Abraham' meant 'Father of many nations'. So now we are going to look at the redemptive names of God and we will begin to see His character through those names.

The seven redemptive names revealing God's character are:

Jehovah Shammah
Jehovah Shalom
Jehovah Jireh
Jehovah Nissi
Jehovah Tsidkenu
Jehovah Rapha
Jehovah Raah

Jehovah Shammah – the Lord or I am there

God is always there. Jesus said, 'Lo, I am with you always.' We need to understand this, because sometimes people think that God has forsaken them. Many times, people will say, 'May God go with you on your holiday.' Well, of course, God will always go with you if He dwells in you. He will always be there.

If people don't feel as if God is with them, they will say, 'God has forsaken me.' No, He hasn't. God said, 'I will never leave you nor forsake you' (Heb. 13.5). It is we who forsake Him.

Many people think that if they want to sin, they go into a bedroom, lock the door, pull the blinds down, and God won't know about it. Your body is the temple of the Holy Spirit who dwells in you; and when you get a revelation of that in your spirit, you won't be able to sin so easily. Because when you are sinning, just imagine what you are doing to the Spirit of God inside you! If God lives in you, He lives in you when you are sinning. That is when we quench the Spirit of God who dwells in us, and we think that God has forsaken us. No, we've forsaken Him. But the Bible says that if you confess your sin, He is faithful and just to forgive you and cleanse you from all unrighteousness (1 John 1.9).

God does not know about our sin when we confess it; He knows about it when we do it. So the sooner we confess it, the sooner we are cleansed of it. Confession is not to inform God about our sins. Many people think that they cannot confess it because then God will find out. No, God knew all the time. But when we confess our sin and ask forgiveness, we are cleansed from all unrighteousness. The door is then closed to the devil. Not only does God forgive us but He forgets.

Kenneth Copeland relates how one day he failed the Lord. That night, in the back of an auditorium filled with thousands of people waiting for him to preach, he was walking up and down talking to the Lord. 'I can't go out there and preach tonight,' he was saying.

The Lord asked him why. And he said, 'Well, you know how I failed you today.'

And the Lord said, 'No, I don't.'

He said, 'What do you mean?'

The Lord said, 'When you confessed it, that's when I forgot it.'

We can stand cleansed by the blood of Jesus when we confess that sin – set free. God not only forgives, but He forgets.

Jehovah Shalom – the Lord our peace

> The chastisement needful to obtain peace was upon Him (Isa. 53.5, Amplified Bible).

That means that Jesus Christ went to the cross, not only for our salvation but also so that we could have peace. All the chastisement needful to obtain peace was put upon Him to enable us to walk in perfect peace. Jesus said, 'My peace I give unto you' (John 14.27), yet many Christians are not walking in peace, either through lack of knowledge or for various other reasons.

> Thou wilt keep him in perfect peace, whose mind is stayed on thee; because he trusteth in thee (Isa. 26.3).

God will keep us in perfect peace, when our mind is stayed on God – on His Word; and the reason why our mind is stayed on Jesus, or the Word, is because we trust in Him. But so many people trust in riches, in circumstances, or in lust of other things and not in God's Word.

Let's reverse Isaiah 26.3 – 'I will not keep you in perfect peace if your mind is not stayed on me because you don't trust in me.' Now, unless your mind is stayed on Jesus Christ and the Word of God, the peace of God will not be made manifest. And one of the biggest hindrances to receiving the peace of God is unbelief. We need to understand that the words 'peace' and 'rest' in the New Testament are interchangeable.

Jesus said in Matthew 11.28, 'Come unto me, all ye that labour and are heavy laden, and I will give you rest [or peace].'

> Let us therefore fear, lest, a promise being left us of entering into his rest [peace], any of you should seem to come short of it. For unto us was the gospel preached, as well as unto them: but the word preached did not profit them, not being mixed with

> faith in them that heard it. For we which have believed do enter into rest [peace], as he said, As I have sworn in my wrath, if they shall enter into my rest [peace]: although the works were finished from the foundation of the world. For he spake in a certain place of the seventh day on this wise, And God did rest the seventh day from all his works. And in this place again, if they shall enter into my rest [peace]. Seeing therefore it remaineth that some must enter therein, and they to whom it was first preached entered not in because of unbelief (Heb. 4.1–6).

You will not enter into the rest and peace of God if you are walking in unbelief; because your mind cannot be stayed on him, and you cannot trust Him if you have unbelief.

> Again, he limiteth a certain day, saying in David, Today, after so long a time; as it is said, Today if ye will hear his voice, harden not your hearts. For if Jesus had given them rest, then would he not afterward have spoken of another day. There remaineth therefore a rest [peace] to the people of God (Heb. 4.7–9).

When I get home after a day under heavy pressure in the ministry, my mind can be racing with questions about the problems I have come across. That is when I have to discipline my mind and concentrate on Jesus. It is such a blessed relief to be able to say, 'Father, I cast the care of the ministry, I cast the care of my job, I cast every care upon You and I am going to sleep.' And then I go to bed and sleep – that is the peace of God.

But many times we cast our cares upon the Lord and then we take them back. We give them to Him, and then we say, 'I don't know how I am going to manage tomorrow.' Well, if we have given Him our cares, then it is His problem – not ours. That takes faith, it is not arrogance or stupidity. It is acting on God's Word, 'casting all your care upon him for he careth for you' (1 Peter 5.7). God wants to take our problems but we must give them to Him.

> For he that is entered into his rest, he also hath cleansed from his own works, as God did from his (Heb. 4.10).

When we try to work everything out ourselves, we will not be able to enter into God's rest. But when we say, 'Father, I can't handle this situation, but You can, so I place this in Your hands and I am going to rest in that,' then the peace of God will come.

> Let us labour therefore to enter into that rest, lest any man fall after the same example of unbelief. For the word of God is quick, and powerful, and sharper than any two-edged sword, piercing even to the dividing asunder of soul and spirit, and of the joints and marrow, and is a discerner of the thoughts and intents of the heart (Heb.4.11–12).

We are to cease from our own works yet we are to labour. But we are to labour in the Word! Labouring in the Word means to put the Word first in every situation. Begin to confess the Word, to live the Word, to act on the Word. That is the labour, but it is also a wonderful rest.

Jehovah Jireh – the Lord will provide

God is our provider. Whenever the Israelites said, 'Jehovah Jireh', they were saying, 'The Lord will provide. God will provide for your every need.'

> My God shall supply all your need according to his riches in glory by Christ Jesus (Phil. 4.19).

Jehovah Nissi – the Lord our victor

We need to understand that Jesus Christ is no longer on the cross; He is a victorious, overcoming God. 'And having spoiled principalities and powers, he made a show of them openly, triumphing over them in it' (Col. 2.15).

He is seated at the right hand of the Father; and He is living in us: 'Greater is he that is in you, than he that is in the world' (1 John 4.4).

Jesus is not on the cross, but He is seated at the right hand of the Father, making intercession for us, and He defeated the devil 2,000 years ago. In Christ we have His authority and His name; He is our victor; He is the champion of our salvation.

Jehovah Tsidkenu – the Lord our righteousness

> For he hath made him to be sin for us, who knew no sin, that we might be made the righteousness of God in him (2 Cor. 5.21).

When we are born again, we are made in right-standing with Jesus Christ. We are made in right-standing with the Holy Spirit and God the Father. We can say, 'I'm a son of the living God, I am a joint heir with Jesus Christ, I've been washed by the blood of the Lamb, and I'm a priest, a king.' And you are in right-standing – not a worm, not the dust of the earth, but a son of the living God. God sees each of us as so valuable and precious that He sent His only begotten Son – for us; that we might be in right-standing with Him. We read in Isaiah 54.17: 'Their righteousness is of me, saith the Lord.'

Jehovah Rapha – the Lord that healeth thee

Healing is just as much part of our salvation as eternal life with God the Father in Heaven.

Every time God says 'Jehovah Rapha', He is saying, 'The Lord that healeth thee.' God is not the One destroying this world. 2 Corinthians 4.4 tells us that Satan is the god of this world. Jesus said:

> The thief cometh not, but for to steal, and to kill, and to destroy: I am come that they might have life, and that they might have it more abundantly (John 10.10).

Many people think that God is controlling everything on

this earth, but if that were true, then God could not be very intelligent. The world is in a mess – we are running short of petrol, there are wars everywhere. Some people have too much food and some people are starving to death. If God is supposed to be responsible for all these things, then He cannot be a great God! But the truth is that Adam was given dominion over the earth and he gave authority to the devil. It is Satan, the god of this world, who is responsible for the mess, and his lease is nearly up. Jesus is coming back soon.

> That it might be fulfilled which was spoken by Esaias the prophet, saying, himself took our infirmities, and bare our sicknesses (Matt. 8.17).

> Who his own self bare our sins in his own body on the tree, that we, being dead to sins, should live unto righteousness; by whose stripes ye were healed (1 Pet.2.24).

There are certain principles that will work for us in the Word if we will apply them in our life. When we find ourselves in an emergency situation, we need to have the Word of God abiding strongly in us.

> My son, attend to my words; incline thine ear unto my sayings, Let them not depart from thine eyes; keep them in the midst of thine heart. For they are life unto those that find them, and health to all their flesh (Prov. 4.20–22).

Jesus and the Word are one. Healing dwells in your spirit: 'He sent his word and healed them' (Ps. 107.20).

Jehovah Raah – our Shepherd

The Lord is my shepherd (Ps. 23.1)
The original Hebrew expresses this verse as 'The Lord my shepherd.' The word 'is' does not appear: that is it reads, 'My shepherd the Lord.' We cannot separate the Shepherd from the Lord or the Lord from the Shepherd. They are one

and the same. The Lord is my Shepherd and my Shepherd is the Lord.

Firstly, we must understand that the subject of the Psalm is the Shepherd, and not David. The emphasis is on the Shepherd, and verses 2 to 6 explain verse 1. These verses show us what a wonderful shepherd the Lord is to us. If Jesus Christ is our Lord, then He is our Shepherd. Many people only allow Jesus to be Lord in certain areas of their lives; but if you really want to know Him as your Shepherd, you have to give Him first place in everything that you do – you have to be saturated with Jesus Christ.

I shall not want (Ps. 23.1)
That simply means we shall not want for anything – we do not lack anything. If God is revealing Himself through being a Shepherd, we need to find out what a shepherd is really like. But most people have the wrong impression of a shepherd; their impression is formed from memories of school nativity plays. The shepherd is normally the little fellow who stands in the corner wearing his daddy's gown which is several sizes too large and he never says a word. He doesn't do anything, he just stands there holding his daddy's walking stick, with a towel wrapped round his head hiding his face!

That is not the Shepherd described in Psalm 23. He defeated the devil 2,000 years ago, and He is looking after us right now.

> I have been young and now am old; yet have I not seen the righteous forsaken, nor his seed begging bread (Ps. 37.25).

This scripture tells us that the Shepherd is looking after us and He knows what we need before we ask Him. (If a person knows what you need before you ask him, he has to be looking at you and watching you. He has to be there. How can he know what you need before you ask, if he is not with you?)

He maketh me to lie down in green pastures (Ps. 23.2)
James chapter 1 tells us why some Christians are not being led by the Spirit of God. If we are led by the Spirit of God, He will always lead us into green pastures. This does not mean that we will never have persecution or affliction – the Word says we will. But the Shepherd is with us to hold our hand – He will lead us out.

He leadeth me beside the still waters (Ps. 23.2)
Jesus never deserts us. He will never forsake us – we forsake Him.

> Fear thou not; for I am with thee: be not dismayed; for I am thy God: I will strengthen thee; yea, I will help thee; yea, I will uphold thee with the right hand of my righteousness. Behold, all they that were incensed against thee shall be ashamed and confounded: they shall be as nothing; and they that strive with thee shall perish (Isa. 41.10–11).

Jesus has given us victory over the enemy, Satan. He shall be as nothing and shall perish.

He restoreth my soul (Ps. 23.3)
I have seen drug addicts get saved and their minds have become normal instantly. A person's soul is his mind and emotions. When we come to Jesus Christ, He makes us completely whole. God will restore our minds and emotions.

He leadeth me in the paths of righteousness for his name's sake (Ps. 23.3)
Our righteousness is of Him. He became sin that we might be made the righteousness of God (2 Cor. 5.21).

Yea, though I walk through the valley of the shadow of death (Ps. 23.4)

We don't stay in the valley, we walk through it; and when we die physically we simply walk on into eternity. A Christian does not experience death after he is born again.

Arthur Blessitt, the man who carries a cross around the world, was on the point of being murdered by a crowd of unbelievers. He said, 'You can't kill me, I died a long time ago. I'll just take a step into eternity.' He knows that he has eternal life; they could not scare him.

Has the shadow of a dog ever bitten anybody? The shadow of death is not death! The devil's best weapon is deceit. He is a master at putting shadows on people. He is a deceiver. How many people have seen a dog's shadow which looks massive? Suddenly the dog comes around the corner, and it is only a tiny little thing but its shadow against the wall made it look huge. That is how Satan operates – he goes around as a roaring lion, but he is actually a mouse with a microphone!

When I was a child, I thought my Dad was the strongest and the most intelligent man in the world. A child thinks his father can do anything. I remember that whenever I got scared, I would run into my parents' bedroom or else they would come into my room if I had a nightmare or was frightened. If the room was dark, I always imagined things, but once the light went on and I had my Daddy with me, there was no problem. We need to get the revelation that our Father God is the best Daddy on this earth, and that He is always with us.

I was in America when I received that revelation, and it was the first time that my wife and I were away from our family. I was working in a health spa, and I didn't have one cent on me. I thought, 'I'm so hungry, if I could just get something to eat.' Then the revelation came. (Now my Father God had spoken to my heart previously and He had said, 'The same as your Daddy has been to you all your life, I will be to you for the rest of your life.') So I simply said,

'Daddy, I need five dollars because I want something to eat. Please can I have it?' I spoke to God like that when there was no one around. Five minutes later someone walked into the gym and said, 'You know, I had forgotten that I borrowed five dollars from you months ago, so here it is.'

Once you get that revelation, you can walk and talk with Him and discuss things with Him. You can sit down and listen to Him. Once God becomes Daddy to you, your whole life will change. The devil has tried to prevent the children of God from having that relationship with their Heavenly Father. Tradition and religion have taught people to be afraid of Him. But our Father loves us more than any earthly father could possibly love us – more than any human being could ever love us. His love is consistent; He gives. His love is not dependent on what it receives – He just gives regardless of what we do or say.

I will fear no evil: for thou art with me (Ps. 23.4)
Wherever we go, if Jesus lives in us, He goes with us; and He is the greatest friend we can ever have. He is our Shepherd.

Thy rod and thy staff they comfort me (Ps. 23.4)
The rod used at that time in Israel was a big stick with a large round knob at the end and the staff was a long stick with a hook at the end. The shepherd used to beat off wild animals that tried to attack his sheep and the staff was used to pull them out of tight spots when they were stuck. The Lord showed me that His rod beats off the enemy, Satan, and His staff hooks us out of tight spots. God is a miracle working God, and He will help us out of a tight spot every time just because of His love and grace.

Thou preparest a table before me in the presence of mine enemies (Ps. 23.5)
We need to realise that every promise and blessing that is in the Bible is there regardless of the circumstances that we

happen to be in. The Lord said to me, 'Cast your cares upon Me for I care for you, rest in Me and walk in My blessings and in My love and in My joy and in My peace.' But many times we say, 'I'm so worried, I can't sleep, what am I going to do about this problem?' Yet God says, 'Don't worry about the attack from the enemy, cast that care on Me. I have prepared a table before you in the midst of your enemies, so sit down and eat, instead of running after the devil, trying to chase him.'

When things seem to be going wrong, relax and say, 'God, I'm going to sleep tonight. I have cast this care upon You and as You never slumber or sleep, there is no need for us both to stay awake.'

Jimmy Swaggart tells this story. He says he was pacing up and down one night saying, 'Lord, I need 80,000 dollars by tomorrow morning otherwise they are going to close my ministry.' He was getting annoyed with his wife who was snoring peacefully because it seemed as though she couldn't care less.

Eventually at about three-thirty in the morning, the Lord said to him, 'Jimmy, how much of the $80,000 can you raise by the morning?'

He said, 'Not a cent.'

God said, 'Well, why don't you just stop worrying and go to sleep?'

Thou anointest my head with oil (Ps. 23.5)
Praise God, the Shepherd heals. We know the Holy Spirit is symbolised by oil – anointing with oil. The Shepherd is the One that fills you with the Holy Spirit.

> Is any sick among you? Let him call for the elders of the church; and let them pray over him, anointing him with oil in the name of the Lord: And the prayer of faith shall save the sick, and the Lord shall raise him up; and if he have committed sins, they shall be forgiven him. Confess your faults one to another, and pray for one another, that ye may be healed (Jas. 5.14–16).

Unforgiveness can hinder your healing but the Shepherd heals through the Holy Spirit.

My cup runneth over (Ps. 23.5)
Malachi 3.10 tells us that the windows of heaven will be opened. Oral Roberts once said, 'Not a trickle, not a stream, not a river, but a flood.'

> Good measure, pressed down, and shaken together, and running over, shall men give into your bosom (Luke 6.38).

Prosperity means to meet any given need at any given time – the word 'rich' means a full supply. (That does not mean that you are going to be a millionaire!) 'Running over' implies abundance so that you can be a blessing to everybody else. When you have more than enough, then you can give. But if you do not have enough, what are you going to give? I want my cup to run over – I want to have enough for everybody around me.

> Wealth and riches shall be in his house, and his righteousness endureth for ever (Ps. 112.3).

A full supply shall be in your house.

Let us look at Luke 15 – the story of the prodigal son. The prodigal son comes back and the father – the Shepherd – is waiting to welcome his beloved son home, the son who had turned his back on his father and left home.

> But the father said to his servants, Bring forth the best robe, and put it on him; and put a ring on his hand, and shoes on his feet: And bring hither the fatted calf, and kill it; and let us eat, and be merry (Luke 15.22–23).

That shows us the Shepherd.

There was another son who saw what happened:

> And he was angry, and would not go in: therefore came his father out, and entreated him. And he answering said to his father, Lo, these many years do I serve thee, neither transgressed I at any time thy commandment; and yet thou never gavest me a kid, that I might make merry with my friends (Luke 15.28).

There are people today who think God does not want them to have anything. They believe it is God's will for them to be poor. Many will say to the Father: 'I served You, I did everything. Why did I never get anything?' Look what the father says to the son:

> And he said unto him, son thou art ever with me, and all that I have is thine (Luke 15.31).

The best robe and the fatted calf had always been his. The Shepherd tells us today, 'What is Mine is thine.' That is our covenant.

God will feed you; He will supply your children with a good education; He will give you the desires of your heart; He will look after you. God will meet your needs. Of course, if there are only two of you, it is no use buying a twelve-roomed house – unless you want to use ten of the bedrooms for people who can't afford to pay rent! But God will supply you with what you need.

Surely goodness and mercy shall follow me all the days of my life (Ps. 23.6)
Goodness and mercy follow the Shepherd, so all we have to do is get in between the Shepherd and the goodness and mercy. When Jesus is ahead of us, and goodness and mercy behind us, the devil doesn't get in too easily.

And I will dwell in the house of the Lord for ever (Ps. 23.6)
If Jesus Christ is the Lord of our life, we will spend eternity with Him. The day we were born again, we received eternal

life. How blessed, how wonderful to spend eternity with Jesus.

7. Abraham – God's friend

The story of Abraham and Isaac has been misrepresented so many times through illustrations, television, movies, etc. Most people have been deceived into believing that God forced Abraham to sacrifice his little child against his will. The picture is painted of a cruel God expecting Abraham to kill his only child for absolutely no reason. One particular movie I saw showed Abraham dragging Isaac along who was crying and screaming at the top of his voice, 'Please don't take me up there.' He would stop every two minutes and say, 'God, don't do this to me.' He would bang his head on the mountainside and attempt to pull out his hair. It took about an hour to get Isaac up the mountain, struggling and shouting all the way.

However, we need to read the Word of God to see the truth. Genesis 22 shows us exactly what happened. Disregard what tradition and religion have taught and simply believe what God's Word tells us.

> And it came to pass after these things, that God did tempt Abraham (Gen. 22.1).

The word 'tempt' means 'test'. God will test your faith because 'the just shall live by faith'. We must live by faith to please God. When we begin to stand on the Word and to walk according to the will of God, God will test our faith.

Someone said, 'I live by faith, Hallelujah, God is my source.' One week later that person is downcast and saying, 'I've lost my job – I don't know what I am going to do.' Who was their source? Their job or God? Living by faith will bring persecution and affliction from the devil. Sometimes God will say to me, 'Give that money you have in your pocket.'

And I say, 'But, God, don't you know that I haven't got any more where this came from?'

But He says, 'Give.'

When you know the character of God and He tells you to give, you realise that if you open that channel, God is going to bless you.

One night at Campmeeting in America, after I had been praying for the sick, someone walked up to me, put something in my hand, and said, 'Brother, God told me to give you this.' It was a man's five-carat diamond ring worth several thousand dollars. (At that time our ministry had just begun in a small theatre in Johannesburg and we had no finances, so I began to imagine all the things the money from the ring could buy.) The following night at Campmeeting in Tulsa, Norval Hayes began to take up an offering.

The Spirit of God said to me, 'Use that ring as seed to plant for your ministry.' God said, 'Go up there and put it in the offering.'

But I just remained seated and said, 'But I can use it – there's so much we need for the ministry.' And I began to make up every excuse I could to avoid putting that ring in the offering. Eventually, I said, 'All right, Lord, I'll give it but let me just tell Lyndie. She must agree with me.'

So I asked Lyndie if I should give the ring and she said, 'They are not asking for rings, they are asking for money!'

So, I said, 'Hallelujah, the Lord is just testing my obedience.' (God will test you in small things first because if you are obedient in small things, you will be obedient in big things.) Anyway, I sat there very relieved and said, 'Praise God!' As I said that, Norval Hayes said, 'The Lord has just told me to tell you to bring your jewellery.'

All the lecturers from Rhema School knew about my ring, and as they saw me going down to put it in the offering, they began to laugh. But I believe that was the seed that was sown for this ministry's finances; and I believe God for a hundred-fold return on that money.

We are told by God to walk by faith and in James 2.23,

He says that Abraham walked by faith and he was called the friend of God.

> And Abraham rose up early in the morning, and saddled his ass, and took two of his young men with him, and Isaac his son, and clave the wood for the burnt offering, and rose up, and went unto the place of which God had told him. Then on the third day Abraham lifted up his eyes, and saw the place afar off. And Abraham said unto his young men, Abide ye here with the ass; and I and the lad will go yonder and worship, and come again to you (Gen. 22.3–5).

He says that *both* of them will come back. Let's refer back to what God told Abraham in Genesis 17.

> And God said, Sarah thy wife shall bear thee a son indeed; and thou shalt call his name Isaac: and I will establish my covenant with him for an everlasting covenant, and with his seed after him (Gen. 17.19).

God's Word was out. Now let's read what Paul says in Hebrews 11.

> By faith Abraham, when he was tried, offered up Isaac: and he that had received the promises offered up his only begotten son, of whom it was said, That in Isaac shall thy seed be called: Accounting that God was able to raise him up, even from the dead; from whence also he received him in a figure (Heb. 11.17–18).

Paul is saying that because God had put His Word out, even if Abraham killed Isaac as a sacrifice, God would have raised him up from the dead. Abraham knew the Covenant he had with Almighty God. One needs to study the Covenant to really understand its meaning. Basically, a covenant is when two people make a solemn pledge to each other, saying, 'What is mine is yours, and what is yours is mine –

all that I have is yours, and all that you have is mine.' That was the Covenant that God made with Abraham. God made that Covenant with His people primarily to get the Messiah into this earth.

> And Abraham took the wood of the burnt offering, and laid it upon Isaac his son; and he took the fire in his hand, and a knife; and they went both of them together. And Isaac spake unto Abraham his father, and said, My father; and he said, Here am I, my son. And he said, Behold the fire and the wood: but where is the lamb for a burnt offering? (Gen. 22.6–7).

When Adam sinned, he gave his authority on this earth to Satan who then became the god of this world (2 Cor. 4.4). But now because of the Covenant with God (what is mine is yours and what is yours is mine), Abraham is willing to give up his son Isaac. If I have a covenant with John (what is his is mine and what is mine is his) and I come to John and say, 'Take your son and do this,' what position does that put me in? I have to do the same with my son! That is what God was doing, that is the way His plan was put into motion and God did that legally. The devil and all his demons could not do anything about it. If Abraham was prepared to sacrifice his son, God could then sacrifice His only Son.

> And Abraham said, My son, God will provide Himself a lamb for a burnt offering: so they went both of them together (Gen. 22.8).

Notice that according to the Word of God there was no negative confession from Abraham. In Mark 5 we can see another man who walked by faith and not by sight, Jairus:

> And besought him greatly, saying, My little daughter lieth at the point of death: I pray thee, come and lay thy hands on her, that she may be healed; and she shall live. And Jesus went with him; and much people followed him, and thronged him. And a cer-

tain woman, which had an issue of blood twelve years, And had suffered many things of many physicians, and had spent all that she had, and was nothing bettered, but rather grew worse, When she had heard of Jesus, came in the press behind, and touched his garment. For she said, If I may touch but his clothes, I shall be whole. And straightway the fountain of her blood was dried up; and she felt in her body that she was healed of that plague. And Jesus, immediately knowing in himself that virtue had gone out of him, turned him about in the press, and said, Who touched my clothes? And his disciples said unto him, Thou seest the multitude thronging thee, and sayest thou, Who touched me? And he looked round about to see her that had done this thing. But the woman fearing and trembling, knowing what was done in her, came and fell down before him, and told him all the truth. And he said unto her, Daughter, thy faith hath made thee whole; go in peace, and be whole of thy plague. While he yet spake, there came from the ruler of the synagogue's house certain which said, Thy daughter is dead: why troublest thou the Master any further? (Mark 5.23–35).

We need to let the Holy Spirit reveal the truth to us in these verses. Imagine Jairus walking along with Jesus, who is going to pray for his daughter and someone comes along and says, 'She's dead, it's all over.' Now he could have reacted by screaming and shouting, 'Oh, God, why did you allow this? Oh, God, couldn't you have got Jesus there in time?' But the Word tells us that Jairus kept silent.

As soon as Jesus heard the word that was spoken, he saith unto the ruler of the synagogue, Be not afraid, only believe. [Jesus made no negative confessions.] And he suffered no man to follow him, save Peter, and James, and John the brother of James. [Jesus only took men of faith in with Him. The others would have been full of unbelief.] And he cometh to the house of the ruler of the synagogue, and seeth the tumult, and them that wept and wailed greatly. [They were already having the funeral – they were wailing.]

And when he was come in, he saith unto them, Why make ye this

> ado, and weep? the damsel is not dead, but sleepeth. And they laughed him to scorn. But when he had put them all out, he taketh the father and the mother of the damsel, and them that were with him, and entereth in where the damsel was lying.

Jesus knew she was dead but He speaks of things that don't exist as though they do; and He chased them out. Sometimes, we have the impression that Jesus walked around barefoot with a little sheep underneath each arm! But He must have walked into the house and said, 'Now everyone, out!' And everyone went out, regardless of what they thought of Him.

> And he took the damsel by the hand and said unto her, Talitha cumi; which is, being interpreted, Damsel, I say unto thee, arise. And straightway the damsel arose, and walked; for she was of the age of twelve years. And they were astonished with a great astonishment (Mark 5.41–42).

We can learn a lesson from Jairus that we need to remain silent if we are not going to say the things that line up with God's Word. Jairus just kept silent.

> And they came to the place which God had told him of; and Abraham built an altar there, and laid the wood in order, and bound Isaac his son, and laid him on the altar upon the wood. And Abraham stretched forth his hand, and took the knife to slay his son. And the angel of the Lord called unto him out of heaven, and said, Abraham, Abraham: and he said, Here am I. And he said, Lay not thine hand upon the lad, neither do thou anything unto him: for now I know that thou fearest God, seeing thou hast not withheld thy son, thine only son from me. And Abraham lifted up his eyes, and looked, and behold, behind him a ram caught in the thicket by his horns; and Abraham went and took the ram, and offered him up for a burnt offering in the stead of his son (Gen. 22.9–13).

And Abraham had said all along that God would provide a lamb. But instead God gave him a ram because the lamb was still to come. I believe that when Abraham lifted up his eyes and looked, he saw the sacrificial lamb, and what was going to take place in time to come. Through Abraham's obedience, he was instrumental in bringing the Messiah, the Saviour of the world, into this earth. In the New Testament, Jesus said,

> Your father Abraham rejoiced to see my day: and he saw it, and was glad (John 8.56).

When Abraham said that God would provide the sacrificial Lamb, it gave God the legal right to send Jesus.

> That in blessing I will bless thee, and in multiplying I will multiply thy seed as the stars of the heaven, and as the same which is upon the sea shore; and thy seed shall possess the gate of his enemies;
>
> And in thy seed shall all the nations of the earth be blessed; because thou hast obeyed my voice.
>
> So Abraham returned unto his young men, and they rose up and went together to Beersheba; and Abraham dwelt at Beersheba (Gen. 22.7–19).

Abraham said, 'We will return' and they did.

The Word tells us in Galatians: 'And if ye be Christ's then are ye Abraham's seed, and heirs according to the promise' (Gal. 3.29).

We are heirs of God's promise to Abraham – Abraham's blessings are ours. We have a Covenant with God and we can stand on that Covenant.

8. Paul's thorn in the flesh

When we preach on divine healing and say that God does not put sickness on people, many immediately say, 'Yes, but what about Paul's thorn?' If the man who wrote two-thirds of the New Testament could not get healed, with all the faith he had, then we certainly have a problem. But we need to read every verse in the Bible in the context of the whole chapter. Originally the Bible was not written in chapter and verse. We must never take one verse out of context – most cults have been built around one particular verse which has been taken out of context.

The Bible does not contradict itself otherwise how would we know whether John 3.16 is true or not? There will always be other verses to back up whatever is written in one particular verse.

> All scripture is given by inspiration of God and is profitable for doctrine, for reproof, for correction, for instruction in righteousness (2 Tim. 3.16).

> Study to show thyself approved unto God, a workman that needeth not to be ashamed, rightly dividing the word of truth (2 Tim. 2.15).

We are now going to examine the Word on Paul's thorn and we will know the truth.

> Bless the Lord, O my soul, and forget not all his benefits: who forgiveth all thine iniquities; who healeth all thy diseases (Ps. 103.2–3).

We need to understand that in the time of Paul, if they were brought up in the Hebrew tradition, by the age of ten years, every Jew should have known the first five books of the Bible off by heart. Paul, in fact, continued his studies under a great scholar, Gamaliel, and he knew almost all the Old Testament off by heart. He knew the Word of God.

> How God anointed Jesus of Nazareth with the Holy Ghost and with power: who went about doing good and healing all that were oppressed of the devil; for God was with him (Acts 10.38).

God is no respecter of persons according to His Word (Acts 10.34). Now my calling might be different to someone else's but God is not a respecter of persons regarding His promises in the Word.

The truth sets us free. So many people say that God has made them ill to teach them something, that it is His will. But Jesus said, 'Let it be done on earth as it is in heaven.' Is there sickness in heaven?

> Persecutions, afflictions, which came unto me at Antioch, at Iconium, at Lystra; what persecutions I endured: but out of them all the Lord delivered me (2 Tim. 3.11).

Delivered him out of them all! In Galatians 3.13 Paul made – under the inspiration of the Holy Spirit – one of the most outstanding statements in the New Testament. He knew what the curse of the law was because by the age of ten years, he would have known off by heart Deuteronomy 28 which tells us what the curse of the law is: 'Christ hath redeemed us from the curse of the law…' (Gal. 3.13).

The curse was threefold – poverty, spiritual death and sickness. Paul told us that Christ had redeemed us from the curse of the law. If a man who knows what the curse of the law is writes, under the inspiration of the Holy Spirit, that Christ has redeemed us from it, then obviously he himself could not have been sick. He had persecutions and afflictions but there is not one mention in the Bible by Paul that he was sick.

Where does your faith begin? Where the will of God is known. If you do not know what God's will is in your life, then you cannot apply faith in that area.

> For let not that man think that he shall receive anything of the Lord. A doubleminded man is unstable in all his ways (Jas. 1.7).

If you are unsure whether you should be sick or well, then you are not going to receive anything from the Lord. That is being doubleminded. A doubleminded man tries to live by faith but protects his fear at the same time.

Many people have said that Paul's sickness was an eye disease which caused pus to flow from a person's eyes continually. These people say that this pus was flowing out of Paul's eyes and he tried to get his healing and God said, 'No, I want you to be like that.' This man travelled extensively preaching the gospel supposedly with pus running down his face all the time!

2 Corinthians tells us of Paul's persecutions and afflictions. We will also receive persecutions and afflictions from the devil but the Bible says:

> For whatsoever is born of God overcometh the world and this is the victory that overcometh the world, even our faith (1 John 5.4).

> Would to God you could bear with me a little in my folly: and indeed bear with me (2 Cor. 11.1).

At that time, everywhere that Paul preached the Word of God, the Judaisers would come in as soon as he moved on, and they would start teaching that only circumcised people could be saved and that they had to adhere to the Jewish law. Now Paul is saying to them, 'You keep on listening to those people. Now I'm going to boast a bit, let me get a bit foolish. Let me tell you what has been happening to me.'

> Wherefore? because I love you not? God knoweth. But what I do, that I will do, that I may cut off occasion from them which desire occasion; that wherein they glory, they may be found even as we. For such are false apostles, deceitful workers, transforming themselves into the apostles of Christ. And no marvel; for Satan himself is transformed into an angel of light (2 Cor. 11.11–14).

Even if 10,000 angels appear to you, if it is not in line with the Word of God, don't be deceived. There is no new revelation. Paul said, 'If any man add or subtract let him be accursed.'

> Therefore it is no great thing if his ministers also be transformed as the ministers of righteousness; whose end shall be according to their works. I say again, Let no man think me a fool; if otherwise, yet as a fool receive me, that I may boast myself a little. That which I speak, I speak it not after the Lord, but as it were foolishly, in this confidence of boasting (2 Cor. 11.15–17).

Paul says in effect, 'Look, I really don't want to tell you everything that has happened to me, but I will anyway.'

> Seeing that many glory after the flesh, I will glory also. For ye suffer fools gladly, seeing ye yourselves are wise. For ye suffer, if a man bring you into bondage, if a man devour you, if a man take of you, if a man exalt himself, if a man smite you on the face. I speak as concerning reproach, as though we had been weak. Howbeit whereinsoever any is bold, (I speak foolishly,) I am bold also. Are they Hebrews? so am I. Are they Israelites? so am I. Are they of the seed of Abraham? so am I. Are they ministers of Christ? (I speak as a fool) I am more; in labours more abundant, in stripes above measure, in prisons more frequent, in deaths oft.

Now Paul speaks of the thorn in his flesh:

> Of the Jews five times received I forty stripes save one. Thrice was I beaten with rods, once was I stoned, thrice I suffered shipwreck, a night and a day I have been in the deep; In journeyings often, in perils of waters, in perils of robbers, in perils by mine own countrymen, in perils by the heathen, in perils in the city, in perils in the wilderness, in perils in the sea, in perils among false brethren; In weariness and painfulness, in watchings often, in hunger and thirst, in fastings often, in cold and nakedness.

> Beside those things that are without, that which cometh upon me daily, the care of the churches. Who is weak, and I am not weak? Who is offended, and I burn not? If I must needs glory, I will glory of the thing which concern mine infirmities (2 Cor. 11.18–30).

Paul says here, 'I have been persecuted, I have been afflicted,' but he also says that in all things he is more than a conqueror (Rom. 8.37) and 'I can do all things through Christ Jesus' (Phil. 4.13).

There are times when we have to exercise our faith; times when we will have to stand on the Word of God. Persecution and affliction will come but circumstances are subject to change when we speak the Word and exercise our faith. Some people think that the day they are born again all their problems cease but sometimes that is when they really begin.

When I started preaching on divine healing, I was about the only person who did not get sick by the following week! Jesus taught His disciples (Mark 4) that the devil comes immediately to steal the Word, because once you get the Word down in your spirit, then he can't steal it. But when you get the revelation of divine healing in your spirit, and you start to meditate and rejoice in what is yours, saying 'Hallelujah, by His stripes I'm healed, He bore my sicknesses, therefore I am healed,' suddenly the flu attacks you worse than ever before. That is the time to confess the Word even more.

Some people think it is not important to believe God for healing for a headache, but that is where your believing should start. When you can get that headache healed by the power of Jesus Christ, then the next time Satan tries to put something on you, you can exercise your faith that much more easily.

Not once in 2 Corinthians 11, when Paul talks about his sufferings and persecutions, does he mention sickness. The same word 'infirmities' is used in Romans 8.26:

> Likewise the Spirit also helpeth our infirmities: for we know not what we should pray for as we ought: but the Spirit itself maketh intercession for us with groanings which cannot be uttered.

It is not sickness, it means 'a weakness or persecution'.

> It is not expedient for me doubtless to glory. I will come to visions and revelations of the Lord. I knew a man in Christ above fourteen years ago, (whether in the body, I cannot tell; or whether out of the body, I cannot tell: God knoweth;) such an one caught up to the third heaven (2 Cor. 12.1–2).

I have prayed for people who love Jesus, who are on their deathbed and they don't want to come back – they have had a glimpse of heaven and they want to go. E. W. Kenyon, one of the great men of faith, walked outside one day, told his family he was going to be with Jesus, sat in his favourite rocking chair and within half an hour, he had left his body and gone. That is the way to go! That is why Paul said he was in a conflict, whether to go and be with Jesus or finish the race he had run here.

> And I knew such a man, (whether in the body, or out of the body, I cannot tell: God knoweth;) How that he was caught up into paradise, and heard unspeakable words, which it is not lawful for a man to utter. Of such an one will I glory: yet of myself I will not glory, but in mine infirmities. For though I would desire to glory, I shall not be a fool; for I will say the truth: but now I forbear, lest any man should think of me above that which he seeth me to be, or that he heareth of me. And lest I should be exalted above measure through the abundance of the revelations... (2 Cor. 12.3–7).

At that time Paul must have been the most dangerous man alive to the devil because he was writing most of the New Testament. The devil had him beaten, stoned, shipwrecked, and did his best to stop him from giving the abundance of revelations he had received from the Lord. When we are full of faith and we begin to do things for God, to cast out devils, to lay hands on the sick and they are healed, the devil will come against us. But each time he comes against us, we should use that as another opportunity to prove God.

> ...there was given to me a thorn in the flesh, the messenger of Satan to buffet me, lest I should be exalted above measure.' [Not a messenger of God.]

Paul took the expression 'a thorn in the flesh' from the Old Testament.

The word *buffet* means 'to strike repeated blows over and over'. Sickness is not 'repeated blows over and over'. The thorn in his flesh was a continuous thing.

Let's look in the Old Testament at the expression Paul used, 'A thorn in the flesh'.

> But if ye will not drive out the inhabitants of the land from before you; then it shall come to pass, that those which ye let remain of them shall be pricks in your eyes, and thorns in your sides, and shall vex you in the land wherein ye dwell (Num. 33.55).

Similarly, today we use the expression 'a pain in the neck'.

The Bible says, 'Out of the mouth of two or three witnesses let every word be established', so let us look at more Scriptures.

> Know for a certainty that the Lord your God will no more drive out any of these nations from before you; but they shall be snares and traps unto you, and scourges in your sides, and thorns in your eyes... (Josh. 23.13).

> But the sons of Belial shall be all of them as thorns thrust away, because they cannot be taken with hands (2 Sam. 23.6).

Three times in the Old Testament 'the thorns' are people.

> For this thing I besought the Lord thrice, that it might depart from me (2 Cor. 12.8).

Paul is saying, in effect, 'God, please do something about these Judaisers, these people who are stoning and beating me, because wherever I go, they are there.'

> And he said unto me, My grace is sufficient for thee: for my strength is made perfect in weakness. Most gladly therefore will I rather glory in my infirmities, that the power of Christ may rest upon me (2 Cor. 12.9).

The sooner we realise that we can do nothing, the sooner God can do everything through us. Some people have said, 'Well, I've tried everything and now I just give up,' and I say, 'Hallelujah, Praise God, now Jesus can do something!'

Sometimes you may think when you turn to Jesus that it is not going to work at first.

A man once gave this testimony. He said he was in serious financial difficulty but he started confessing (Phil. 4.19) 'My God shall supply all my need according to his riches in glory by Christ Jesus.' He kept confessing this but then he thought he should go down to the bank just in case! So he arrived at this huge bank and his confession grew smaller and smaller. The more he looked at the huge bank, the smaller his confession seemed. But he made a decision to stand on the Word and he turned and left the bank, and God performed a miracle in his life. He said that when he went back into that bank, his confession 'My God shall supply all my need,' seemed twice the size of the bank.

When you realise you can do nothing, then Jesus will do it through you. If I laid hands on the sick in my own strength, they would not recover, but if I lay hands on the sick in the name of Jesus, then they will.

> Therefore I take pleasure in infirmities, in reproaches, in necessities, in persecutions, in distresses for Christ's sake: for when I am weak, then am I strong (2 Cor. 12.10).

When we depend on the Spirit of God, we are more than conquerors through Christ. When we depend on Jesus, we can do all things through Christ Jesus. All things are possible to them that believe. I am a world overcomer because I walk by faith and not by sight. I am born of God. Greater is He that is in me than he that is in the world.

The Body of Christ is getting into the position where they realise who they are in Christ. They are beginning to walk in the knowledge of who they are in Christ. Not only do we need to have the revelation of what Christ did for us, but also the revelation of who we are right now.

Another argument people have against divine healing is from Galatians 4. Paul states:

> Ye know how through infirmity of the flesh I preached the gospel unto you at the first. And my temptation which was in my flesh ye despised not, nor rejected; but received me as an angel of God, even as Christ Jesus. Where is then the blessedness ye spake of? For I bear you record, that, if it had been possible, ye would have plucked out your own eyes, and have given them to me (Gal. 4.13–15).

So people say, 'You see, look at this scripture. Paul had problems with his eyes and when he went to preach at first in Derbe he had that sickness.'

Let us now see where Paul first went to Derbe. Derbe, Iconium, Antioch and Lystra, were cities in the province of Galatia.

> They were aware of it, and fled unto Lystra and Derbe, cities of Lycaonia and unto the region that lieth round about: And there they preached the gospel.

> And there sat a certain man at Lystra impotent in his feet, being a cripple from his mother's womb, who never had walked: The same heard Paul speak: who steadfastly beholding him, and perceiving that he had faith to be healed, Said with a loud voice, Stand upright on thy feet. And he leaped and walked (Acts 14.6–10).

How do you get healed? Faith cometh by hearing and hearing about healing. Paul is preaching the Word of God (I believe he must have been preaching healing) and this man is sitting there crippled, listening to Paul, who says, 'I perceive you have faith to be healed, get up and walk' and the man gets up and walks. How convincing would Paul have been, preaching on divine healing, while he was obviously suffering from an eye disease himself? The Scripture continues, saying that they began to worship Paul and Barnabas.

> And there came thither certain Jews from Antioch and Iconium [the thorn in the flesh] who persuaded the people, and having stoned Paul, drew him out of the city, supposing he had been dead (Acts 14.19).

They stoned Paul to death for healing a crippled man. He was preaching the gospel with power and revival came to that town, so Satan came, bringing persecution immediately. I believe Paul actually died and that was when he was caught up into the third heaven, and I believe that the disciples gathered around him, laid hands on him, prayed and he rose up healed. We are told that the very next day he went back into the town and preached the gospel. Now even though he was healed, don't you think his face would have been battered, particularly his eyes, when he was stoned? No wonder the people wanted to give him their own eyes! This account in Acts is telling us about the time he preached at the first in Galatia.

Paul said he had fought the good fight of faith. A good fight is a fight where you win. Have you ever heard a boxer who has been knocked out, saying afterwards that it was a good fight?

> For I am now ready to be offered, and the time of my departure is at hand. I have fought a good fight, I have finished my course, I have kept the faith: Henceforth there is laid up for me a crown of righteousness, which the Lord, the righteous Judge, shall give me at that day: and not to me only, but unto all them also that love his appearing (2 Tim. 4.6–8).

9. The reality of God in our lives

> And what agreement hath the temple of God with idols? for ye are the temple of the living God; as God hath said, I will dwell in them, and walk in them; and I will be their God, and they shall be my people. Wherefore come out from among them, and be ye separate, saith the Lord, and touch not the unclean thing; and I will receive you, And will be a Father unto you, and ye shall be my sons and daughters, saith the Lord Almighty (2 Cor. 6.16–18).

God says 'I will dwell in them.' We must become God inside-minded. The greatest truth that there is, is that Jesus Christ comes to live in you when you receive Him as Lord and Saviour. Many people will agree and say, 'Yes, I believe that Jesus Christ has come to dwell in me,' yet they are afraid of the dark, they are afraid of the next door neighbour's dog, afraid of everything that moves. Some people have said, 'Oh, I couldn't go and lay hands on someone for healing.' Yet Jesus is dwelling in them! No person can do any healing anyway, it is only Jesus in that person who will heal someone. We need to stop worrying about our own reputation, and our own ego, and let Jesus live through us.

Let us look again at John 10.10:

> The thief cometh not, but for to steal, and to kill, and to destroy: I am come that they might have life, and that they might have it more abundantly.

The Greek word translated as 'abundant life' actually means 'superabundant in quantity and superior in quality'.

> Greater is he that is in me than he that is in the world (1 John 4.4).

> I am crucified with Christ: nevertheless I live; yet not I, but Christ liveth in me: and the life which I now live in the flesh I live by the faith of the Son of God, who loved me, and gave himself for me (Gal. 2.20).

It is not enough just to know that Jesus lives in you – you have to let Him walk through you. Some people criticise and say, 'Who do you think you are, walking around like a little Jesus?' Well, what does 'Christian' mean? 'A little anointed one.'

We need to die to ourselves and let Jesus Christ manifest Himself through us. When Jesus begins to walk through you, then the blind will see, the deaf will hear, and the love of God will flow from you. That is why Jesus said, 'You are the light that lighteth up this world, the salt of the earth' (Matt. 5.13–14).

People say, 'How can you talk to things and confess the Word of God over them?' But those same people will talk to their washing machine when it won't work, or to their car when it won't go! Or, they will say, 'Keys I can never find you when I want you!' Or, 'Traffic lights, why are you always red when I'm in a hurry?'

But the time is coming when more people are going to let Jesus walk through them, talk through them, reach out to the lost through them. We should not just reach out for healing for ourselves, but we should be wearing the garment of healing for others. We need to be blessed in order to be a blessing.

For Jesus to walk through us, we have to walk by faith and not by sight. To walk by faith is to walk by God's Word and not by your natural senses. It is a way of life. It is not a 'Get Rich Quick' scheme. It is not just something you do on Sunday morning. It is a twenty-four hour day way of life. God is a faith God and for Him to manifest Himself through you, you have to live by faith.

> If ye abide in me, and my words abide in you, ye shall ask what ye will, and it shall be done unto you (John 15.7).

(Once His Word is abiding in you, His will and your will become one. You won't be asking for something silly or wrong. Once His Word is in you, you know His will because His will is His Word. But most times people don't know what God's Word says, and sometimes people hear things from first imaginations!)

> Herein is my Father glorified, that ye bear much fruit; so shall ye be my disciples (John 15.8).

You may be criticised for being fanatical about the Word of God but being filled with the joy of the Lord is sufficient reward. Many years ago the charismatic movement was not popular; to be a Pentecostal was frowned upon. But now the most prominent people are confessing on television and radio that Jesus Christ is their Lord and Saviour. Top businessmen are confessing Jesus as their Lord. TV actors are witnessing for Jesus, and people in the world are at last beginning to see the abundant life in Jesus. It is only when Christians are walking in that abundant life, that unbelievers are going to want Jesus – they will want that same abundant life. But the Christians who look as if they have been sucking lemons all day are not going to draw people to Jesus. The unbelievers say, 'Look, I've got enough problems of my own already.' People are beginning to see that we have superabundant quantity of life shining from us and It is superior in quality to anyone outside of Jesus Christ.

Even if you already have Jesus in you, you still need to let Him have His way in your life.

Let us look again at 2 Corinthians 6.18: 'And will be a Father unto you, and ye shall be my sons and daughters, saith the Lord Almighty.'

God takes that sinful nature, He makes that sinner a brand new creature in Christ when he comes to Jesus. No longer is he unworthy, no longer is he just the dust of the earth, but he becomes a son of the living God. He makes him a son, a joint heir with Christ, a priest, a king, seated in heavenly places.

When the unbeliever begins to see the joy, the peace, the light and the love flowing from us, he will want what we have. People are coming to the Church all over the world in these last days and finding the truth. There is a hunger and thirst for the light because light dispels darkness.

Many times the problem is that we do not want to completely give all our life to Jesus. I am crucified with Jesus, my old self does not exist any more. Jesus in me is the One who lives now.

Not only did God make us sons and daughters, but He gave us the name of Jesus. Every knee in heaven and earth has to bow to that name (Phil. 2.10).

> And Jesus came and spake unto them, saying, All power is given unto me in heaven and in earth (Matt. 28.18).

> And these signs shall follow them that believe; In my name shall they cast out devils; they shall speak with new tongues; They shall take up serpents; and if they drink any deadly thing, it shall not hurt them; they shall lay hands on the sick, and they shall recover (Mark 16.17–18).

Oral Roberts tells this story. His son went to California – he wanted to make it on his own, and after working there for a year, he went to the Bank for a loan. He went into the manager's office, and said, 'Sir, I've been working here in California for a year now and I would like to have a loan. I've done well, I've banked here and I would like to borrow some money from this Bank.'

The manager said, 'I cannot give you a loan, you have no credentials or security. I don't know who you are or where you come from.'

So the son said, 'Well, my father is Oral Roberts.'

The bank manager immediately said, 'Why didn't you tell me that in the first place? You can have as much as you want.'

> The Spirit itself beareth witness with our spirit that we are the children of God: And if children, then heirs, heirs of God, and joint heirs with Christ; if so be that we suffer with him, that we may be also glorified together (Rom.8.16–17).

You may not feel like a son or daughter at times but God sees you that way when you are born again. God's love is always consistent.

> To redeem them that were under the law, that we might receive the adoption of sons. And because ye are sons, God hath sent forth the Spirit of his Son into your hearts, crying, Abba, Father. Wherefore thou art no more a servant, but a son; and if a son, then an heir of God through Christ (Gal. 4.5–7).

> ...because as he is, so are we in this world (1 John 4.17).

That means Jesus lives in us. I will do anything and go anywhere for Jesus, because of what He did for me.

> Behold, what manner of love the Father hath bestowed upon us, that we should be called the sons of God (1 John 3.1).

We have the capacity to love because Jesus Christ lives in us. Stephen proved that; he learnt how to love when he was serving at tables. When they stoned him, he was able to react with the same love that Jesus had, and say, 'Lord, lay not this sin to their charge.' We need to love others, we need to let the love of God flow through us. Love is all important. Whether or not someone is a great man of faith, if he has not love, then he has nothing (1 Cor. 13). The love of God is shed abroad in our hearts (Rom. 5.5) because we are sons and daughters of the living God.

2
The faithfulness of God

Let us look at the faithfulness of God, because, when you see how faithful God is, you begin to respond and to be faithful, as He is. Paul said: 'Follow me as I follow Christ.' The reason, I believe, that God wants us to see His faithfulness, is because we are often tempted to doubt His faithfulness, and when we do, we get discouraged, and into a position where we think, 'I just do not know if I can really depend on God or His Word.'

Faithfulness is one of the most important attributes of God: for God to be unfaithful, He could not be God. It would be contrary to His nature to be unfaithful.

> Know therefore that the LORD thy God, he is God, the faithful God, which keepeth covenant and mercy with them that love him and keep his commandments to a thousand generations (Deut. 7.9).
>
> It is of the LORD's mercies that we are not consumed, because his compassions fail not. They are new every morning: great is thy faithfulness (Lam. 3.22–23).

God has laid it on my heart to show you some areas where He is faithful, because I believe that there are many who have begun to doubt the faithfulness of God in certain situations.

1. Faithfulness in giving a harvest

The first area in which God will always be faithful, is the area of seedtime and harvest, or sowing and reaping.

Sometimes you feel that you have sown so much love upon someone that you have no more love to give and you are not getting back what you thought you would. At other times it might just have been the seed of kindness that you have sown, but you do not see the harvest. You might have given patience and longsuffering, meekness or even money. You have said: 'Lord, I have given; I have given of myself, I have given with the right motive, I have given in love; I have sown and sown, and yet, Lord, maybe I will not receive a harvest.' You might have sown a seed to get people saved; you might have spoken to your relatives, your family, to your business associates, people you are coming into contact with daily, and you have sown that seed. The Bible tells me that if you have sown, somebody else will water it, and God will give the increase. Do not ever get discouraged; I do not know how long it is going to take, but God's Word never returns empty.

It happened to us with our next-door neighbours: we had sown and sown but they seemed to ignore everything we said about the Bible. Just when we started thinking we had sown enough seed and that something ought to be happening, my friend Brian Gibson came to stay with us for a weekend. The neighbour spoke to Brian about everyday things across the fence, and then Brian grabbed his guitar and went over to the neighbour's house. We did not want to discourage him, so we did not tell him that he was wasting his time, that we had been sowing for three years and nothing had happened; we just left him. Well, Brian went there and within five minutes he had them saved: that is what I mean by someone watering and God giving the increase.

> While the earth remaineth, seedtime and harvest, and cold and heat, and summer and winter, and day and night shall not cease (Gen. 8.22).

In God's work there are two areas of sowing – the natural and the spiritual realm. In the natural realm it might often look as if you have been wasting your time. It might look as if God has not been as faithful as He is supposed to be. Some people start to give, and, if they do not see results in five minutes, they think that it does not work. Some people say: 'Oh, that sounds good, I'll try this.' They try it, but they do not do it; they try it and two days later they say: 'No, that's not for me!' There is a difference between doing it and trying it. As soon as you start tithing you will think that it is the worst thing that you have ever done: all hell normally breaks loose when people start tithing for the first time. But God is faithful to His Word every time: if you have sown, you will harvest; especially if you have sown love in your family. Do you know that the Bible says love will never fail?

Sometimes you might think people in the world are better off, until you sit down and get to know them for half an hour and then you find out that their lives are in a mess.

Paul wrote: 'Be not deceived; God is not mocked: for whatsoever a man soweth, that shall he also reap' (Gal. 6.7). Now, that sounds dangerous for someone who lived a life like I did before I was born again; but when you are born again, your whole past life is forgiven and forgotten. You are not reaping what you sowed before you were born again: any man who is in Christ becomes a new creature. If you sinned and repented of it, then God has forgiven you, but if you did not repent and ask for forgiveness and live for God, you are going to reap what you are sowing.

Many people have been deceived into thinking that they are reaping what they sowed before they were saved. If you are born again and the devil comes to you in any form to tell you that you are now going to reap what you sowed before you were saved, just laugh at him and tell him that you know he is trying to deceive you, and that the man who sowed those seeds died a long time ago; you are a new creature, old things have passed away. You are in Christ, and there is no condemnation in Christ Jesus.

> For he that soweth to his flesh shall of the flesh reap corruption, but he that soweth to the Spirit shall of the Spirit reap life everlasting (Gal. 6.8).

Some of us only want the Word of God to work when it suits us. We want to sow and to reap what suits us. Well, reaping and sowing will work for you in giving, in finances and everything, but it will also work in a sinful life – it is a spiritual law. You see, God is faithful; He is faithful in everything.

2. Faithfulness in fulfilling His Word

> God is not a man, that he should lie; neither the son of man, that he should repent: hath he said, and shall he not do it? or hath he spoken, and shall he not make it good? (Num. 23.19).

Hallelujah, you should get excited about that, because God does not lie, and what His Word says you are, you are; what His Word says you can do, you can do. We can be assured that God is faithful to produce whatever He promised in His Word: He is committed. He said it and therefore He will do it for us. The Bible is true, no matter how vehemently some people try to deny it or prove it wrong; it is God speaking to us, and it will work if you apply it to your life.

> So shall my word be that goeth forth out of my mouth: it shall not return unto me void, but it shall accomplish that which I please, and it shall prosper in the thing whereto I sent it (Isa. 55.11).

God is faithful to back up His Word and to make it prosper in whatever it says it shall do. God and His Word are one and you cannot separate the two: most people who have a problem with God's Word are people who do not give the light of the Spirit to the Word. You see, the Law kills, but the Spirit gives life. If people would allow the Holy Spirit to give life to that Word and allow that Word to begin to become alive and to produce, it will bring results in their lives. You see, if you are just repeating the Word in parrot fashion, it is not God speaking to you. The Bible becomes God speaking to you when it comes into your spirit and becomes a revelation to you, a reality in your life and, as you begin to release that Word, it is really God's Word with faith in it.

The Bible is God's integrity. How good would a man be if he could not be faithful to his word? Suppose I wrote you a letter and said that I would come and pick you up at eight o'clock in the morning and take you on holiday, and the next day, as you stood waiting for me, in anticipation of our holiday, I came driving by and just shouted at you: 'Hey, I am me and I am not coming, goodbye.' You would not be able to trust me, would you? Well, that is what people say God does – they say He can do what He likes. No, He cannot: there are certain things that He cannot do, because He is committed to His Word, and also, He cannot lie. The Psalmist says:

> For ever, O Lord, thy word is settled in heaven (Ps. 119.89).

Did you know that Jesus Himself staked His life on the Word of God? When He was in the wilderness and tempted by the devil, He did not say: 'Well, Mr Devil, man wrote the Bible and you know it was just made up out of man's head. It is just some fanciful story and, in any case, everyone has got his own interpretation of it, so let us just forget about the Bible, I will fight you hand to hand!'

No! He said: 'It is written!' If Jesus staked His walk with God on the Word of God and let the Word of God back Him up when He stood face to face with the devil, then that is what I am going to do. We can stop running away and turn and face the devil and say: 'It is written!'

A while ago I was a guest on a television programme and one of the people who appeared on the panel with me said the Bible was not true, we have just made it up through the ages. I said: 'Well, then we are in real trouble, because then Jesus had vain imaginations when He said that man shall not live by bread alone, but by every word that proceedeth out of the mouth of God.'

I do not think that the devil is all that brilliant, but I do not think that he is that dumb either, that when Jesus said: 'It is written...', if the devil knew that the Bible was not true, he would have replied: 'Don't tell me that it is written, you people have just made that up.'

3. Faithfulness in delivering us from Satan

God is faithful to keep us from the evil one and faithful to help us overcome him. Sometimes in the past we have given the devil more respect and credit than has ever been due to him. Kenneth Hagin was preaching during a flu epidemic once and eventually everybody except he and three other preachers were sick. One of them said to Brother Hagin that it looked as if they were the last ones left, to which he replied: 'Yes, and I am not going to get sick.'

The man said, 'Shh, don't say that so loudly.' When Brother Hagin asked why not, he replied: 'The devil might hear you.'

Now, firstly, no matter how softly you say it, the devil is going to hear you, and, secondly, he is the very one who should hear it. If the devil is starting to put the symptoms of a disease on me, I do not have to convince God about the condition that I am in: I want to convince the devil that I know that the Word of God is true, that I am standing on the Word and that the devil is a liar. He is the one whom I want to hear me saying it – I am talking to him, I am telling him to take his dirty hands off God's property.

> But the Lord is faithful, who shall establish you, and keep you from evil (2 Thess. 3.3).

Many people think that the devil can just come along and do what he wants to you; but you actually have to give him the space, the opportunity and the place to do what he wants to do to you. If you are walking according to God's Word, he has no way of taking advantage of you.

> My sheep hear my voice, and I know them, and they follow me (John 10.27).

Jesus is talking about your spirit. We do not have a problem with our spirits, we have a problem with our heads. If your spirit had its way, you would know God's voice every time; but the trouble is that your spirit does not have its way most of the time, your head and flesh do.

> And I give unto them eternal life; and they shall never perish, neither shall any man pluck them out of my hand. My Father, which gave them to me, is greater than all; and no man is able to pluck them out of my Father's hand (John 10.28–9).

God is faithful to keep you; He will keep you in a place where the devil cannot come and hurt you. God is faithful, and wherever He leads you, He will keep you, so make sure that you stay within His perfect will – let Him show you the place where He wants to keep you. Do not try and force God to adapt to your will, ask Him to lead you to the place that He has prepared for you.

Let us look at how the Amplified Bible translates 1 Corinthians 10.13:

> For no temptation – no trial regarded as enticing to sin (no matter how it comes or where it leads) – has overtaken you and laid hold on you that is not common to man…'

Whatever happens to you, you are not the only one whom it has ever happened to. Some people say that God does not really know what is going on. I have news for them: He does and you are not the only one on the face of the earth who has been through it.

> …that is, no temptation or trial has come to you that is beyond human resistance and that is not adjusted and adapted and belonging to human experience, and such as man can bear. But God is faithful (to His Word and to His compassionate nature) and He (can be trusted) not to let you be tempted and tried and assayed beyond your ability and strength of resistance and power to endure, but with the temptation He will (always) also provide the way out…

If you cannot find a way out of your trials, it is your problem, not God's: He has already provided it, it is your duty to pray for Him to open your eyes and let you see the way you should take to get out of it. Not only has He provided a way out of every test and trial for you, but He is not the one who is doing the testing and trying. How can He be the one who is trying you when it is He who is going to deliver you out of the very same trials? He is not sitting up there playing some computer game with us, to see who will be able to get out of a new little game that He has just thought up.

> …He will (always) also provide the way out – the means of escape to a landing place – that you might be capable and strong and powerful patiently to bear up under it.

Whatever the devil is bringing against and across the paths of the people who are faithful, God will give you a landing place and God is making you strong and patient to bear up under it, and He will give you a way out and you will be able to walk over the devil in every area.

God is faithful to do it; moreover, the Bible says that persecution arises for the Word's sake: you will be tested and tried for the Word's sake (that cannot possibly come from God – why would He put hindrances in the way of the Word?) but God will always provide a way out, and He will give you the strength to stand firmly on His Word.

4. Faithfulness in forgiving us

God is faithful to forgive you. Ninety-nine per cent of people who backslide do it because they run from God instead of towards Him when they have done something wrong. You cannot run away from God and the sooner you repent and go on for God, the quicker your fellowship with Him will be able to get stronger and He will be able to bless you.

> If we confess our sins, he is faithful and just to forgive us our sins, and to cleanse us from all unrighteousness (1 John 1.9).

If you confess your sin and walk with a pure heart before Him; if you let Him be Lord of your life in every area, you walk in total forgiveness, whether you have sinned knowingly or unknowingly. That is the good news, that is the gospel of the Lord Jesus Christ, that God did not love you because of who you were or are, He loves you in spite of who you are or who you were. If you live for Jesus you do not want to sin, you want to please him – that is the motive that will keep you living the right life; not thinking that God is going to hit you on the head every time you do something wrong.

God wants us to live the right life, because the wages of sin are death, and that is not what God wants us to earn. You know, people will complain if they get paid less than they think they should, but the people in the world, who are living without God, will have to be satisfied with the wages of death, because that is what they will be paid for a whole life of sin: death as opposed to eternal life with God. That is what the Bible says and God is faithful to His Word.

> I call heaven and earth to record this day against you, that I have set before you life and death, blessing and cursing: therefore choose life, that both thou and thy seed may live (Deut. 30.19).

> For the wages of sin is death; but the gift of God is eternal life through Jesus Christ our Lord (Rom. 6.23).

5. Faithfulness in saving us and giving us eternal life

God is always faithful to save all who come to Jesus and make Him the Lord of their lives. We often get criticised for the term 'born again': people seem to think that Rhema Ministries of Kenneth Hagin or John G. Lake or John Wesley made that term up; but Jesus used it when He spoke to Nicodemus. He said, 'Ye must be born again' (John 3.7). What often happens, unfortunately, is that the church removes itself so far from the teachings of Jesus that, when you repeat a statement that Jesus first made they think you are making it up.

The book of Acts tells us that the church was added to daily. To me it means that at least 365 people should be saved in any given church in a year, if that church wants to stay with the master plan of the church that was given to us in the book of Acts. It also means that you should give the people the opportunity to be born again every time that you have a service. And God is faithful that the gospel will be preached to all nations through this earth; not religion, not tradition, but the gospel of Jesus Christ, the good news for everyone to hear.

Let us look at John's gospel again:

> Whosoever believeth in him should not perish, but have eternal life. For God so loved the world, that he gave his only begotten Son, that whosoever believeth in him should not perish, but have everlasting life. For God sent not his Son into the world to condemn the world; but that the world through him might be saved (John 3:15–17).

That should give you an answer to the question why some people are not getting anybody saved: they preach that God is going to get you, you had better get saved before you leave here and get run over by a truck. That is not good news; you might still get a few results by trying to scare people into the kingdom, but it is not good news. We should tell people the good news, and this is it; this is why Jesus came: 'For God sent not his Son into the world to condemn the world; but that the world through him might be saved.'

> He that believeth in him is not condemned: but he that believeth not is condemned already, because he hath not believed in the name of the only begotten Son of God. And this is the condemnation, that light is come into the world, and men loved darkness rather than light, because their deeds were evil (John 3.18–19).

Now, you can come to Him just as you are, no matter what your past is like, no matter how you have slipped up, no matter what your abilities or inabilities are. You do not have to go and fix anything up in your life before you come to Him as some people think they must do: without Him you will never get it fixed, anyhow. Come to Him as the prostitute did during His earthly ministry, like all the people did, come remembering that He said He did not come for the healthy but for the sick. Who are the sick? They are those without Jesus. They are the ones He came for, the ones who need to be healed and delivered. The issue is not whether you are good, or what you think, or what your interpretation of anything is

– when you stand before God one day, the issue is going to be: 'What have you done with Jesus? What have you done about Him in your life? Did you allow Him into your life, to change it, so that you can live for Him, or did you ignore Him and did you prefer to live in the darkness of this world?'

If Jesus is not the issue, then it means that you can just be nice and good and get to heaven, and if that was the case, then why did God have to send Jesus to the earth? The Bible says that all have sinned and come short of the glory of God; that is why He had to send Jesus. You could not, by your own works, ever earn salvation: it is a gift. Your works are as filthy rags before the Holiest of Holies of God, in His presence.

Without Jesus you cannot stand in the presence of God. God's glory shines through the heavens; it will kill darkness if it should come into touch with it. With darkness you cannot come into the light. In the Old Testament they just touched the ark and fell down dead. It happened because they came into the presence of God in the nature they were in: sinful, without a mediator. They could not stand and live in His nature, but when you go to heaven with Jesus you are a new creature, recreated; you are just like Him. You will be able to dance and sing and talk to the Lord, because He is faithful, He has promised it to us in His Word, and He is faithful to do it. You can put your trust in His faithfulness today and know that He will do everything that He has promised. Hallelujah.

6. Faithfulness in giving us life in heaven

God is faithful. He is faithful in what He said heaven is like. If you study the book of Revelation, you will find that there are certain descriptions of heaven; for instance, that the streets are made of gold, and the gates of one big pearl.

Well, when we get to heaven we are going to recognise it from those descriptions; we are not going to get up there and think what a strange place this is, we will know where we are from the descriptions of heaven that we have read. Although it will be far better than we can imagine, we will still recognise it as our eternal home.

You have life in heaven if you are born again; it is yours. All that you will stand before him for, will be for God to tell you what blessings and rewards you are going to get, or whether you will not get any. You have passed from death into life, you are not condemned because you have the life and the light of Jesus in you. You will never have to face death; you were once dead, but now you are alive in Jesus Christ. When your earthly life is over, you will simply take off your earthsuit and go on to heaven and live with Jesus. I call your body an earthsuit because you need it only in order to walk this earth, in the same way as a spaceman needs a spacesuit to be able to exist in outer space: but the spacesuit is not the man, just like you are not the body that you can see. You are a spirit, with a mind (or soul) who lives in a body – the spirit part is the important part; that is the part that will live for ever. Yes, everyone will live for ever, whether born again or not; the question for you is, where are you going to spend eternity? If you are not born again, you will be judged and condemned and you will not spend eternity with God. Born-again people will be judged only on what God called them to do, and how they lived up to that; according to that you will receive your rewards.

I believe that the greatest thing that could ever happen to anyone is to get before the Master one day and bow before Him and hear him say, 'Well done, thou good and faithful servant.' That will be far better than anything anyone will ever experience for all eternity.

7. Faithfulness in keeping his promise to come again

God is faithful to back up every prophecy, every word that is in the Book of Revelation and the rest of the Bible that is prophetic and is still to come.

> For this is my blood of the new testament, which is shed for many for the remission of sins. But I say unto you, I will not drink henceforth of this fruit of the vine, until that day when I drink it new with you in my Father's kingdom (Matt. 26.28–9).

God is faithful to the fact that the day will come when the heavens will open, the trumpet will sound and Jesus will come and take us back with Him to have the feast of the Lamb.

Can you imagine living for eternity? Just disappearing from here, meeting Jesus in the air and living for ever with Him and the Father in heaven? God is faithful to do it and we can have a little bit of heaven right here on earth, being led by His Spirit and living in line with His Word, having the peace that passes all understanding. He is faithful to do that for us.

3
Ruling over life's problems

As we study the Word of God, we find the answers to questions concerning our everyday lives and our walk with the Lord Jesus Christ.

Many times when people in the church have asked questions, they have received frustrating replies. As when a child's father says, 'Now, son, don't do that,' and when the child asks, 'Why not?' he is told, 'Because I said so.'

Similarly, the church leaders have said, 'You must do this and you must do that.' The people have asked, 'Why?' and the reply has been, 'Because we say so.'

We want to know how the Word works, how to take it into our lives and homes, into our families, into our everyday lives and we want to know *how* the Bible and our walk with the Lord Jesus Christ is going to benefit us and *why* it works for us right now in this life. The Bible not only talks about the blessings of God in heaven, it talks about us having the blessings of God right here on earth – not only the pie in the sky, but the steak on the plate! A little bit of heaven on earth because we have been translated into the kingdom of His dear Son *right now*. We are not going to be, we are right now in the kingdom of God and we can live according to kingdom rights. We can live according to kingdom principles. We can live this day according to the Word of God and not have to be dominated, defeated or led astray by the devil.

1. Depression and oppression

> Looking unto Jesus the author and finisher of our faith (Heb. 12.2).

> Be ye followers of me, even as I also am of Christ (Paul, in 1 Cor. 11.1).

So many of us are following people or circumstances and we are talking about things that are not really in the Word of God when we need to look to Jesus. *He is the One we are to look to today.*

Many people have the religious idea that Jesus Christ walked on this earth, victorious, and doing all the things that He did because He was God. Now He was God and will always be God, but the Bible tells us that when He walked on this earth, He emptied Himself and became a man. He operated as a prophet under the Old Testament. If He had not walked on this earth as you and I do, then He could not have made the statement 'These works you shall do and greater works' (John 14.12). The Word says, 'How God anointed Jesus of Nazareth with the Holy Ghost' (Acts 10.38). As a man, Jesus had to wait until the age of thirty years before God anointed Him for the ministry He was called into.

If He walked on this earth as God, He could not have been our substitute.

> But made himself of no reputation, and took upon him the form of a servant, and was made in the likeness of men: And being found in fashion as a man, he humbled himself, and became obedient unto death, even the death of the cross (Phil. 2.7–8).

He took upon Himself the form of a servant and was made in the likeness of men. Now the reason why I am making this point is that we need to see that if Jesus Christ, while

He was on this earth, could do it and we now have Jesus living in us, we can do it today.

> For we have not an high priest which cannot be touched with the feeling of our infirmities; but was in all points tempted like as we are, yet without sin (Heb. 4.15).

In every conceivable way that mankind has been tempted, Jesus was also tempted. Now if someone offered me a cigarette, it would not be a temptation as I have never had the desire to smoke. But we are told that Jesus was tempted in every way but was without sin. He had to fight that temptation. He had the temptation of women around Him all the time while He was ministering and He had to exercise His authority and dominion. He had to walk in the spirit. He had the devil trying to trip Him up everywhere He went – trying to have Him thrown off a cliff, tempting Him when He had not eaten for forty days by talking about food. In every way the second Adam was tempted, much more than the first Adam, but the Bible says without sin.

Jesus ruled over every circumstance and problem of life. He ruled over hate – He prayed for His executioners and the Pharisees and said, 'Father, forgive them.' Therefore we should be able to forgive others. We have the life of God in us – Jesus is living in us. The Bible says that the love of God is shed abroad in our hearts.

Jesus ruled over rejection. Peter denied Him and Judas betrayed Him. He ruled over His mind – the devil attacked Him in the wilderness and He came out victorious. He ruled over fear, unbelief and depression.

He had an opportunity to be depressed. He preached the most anointed sermon in the history of mankind when He said that the acceptable year of the Lord had come (Luke 4.19). (Leviticus chapter 25 explains the acceptable year of the Lord.) He said the poor do not have to be poor any more – that is the good news. The broken hearted can be set free, the ones who are captive do not have to be captive any more. I can imagine Him reading from the book of Isaiah and at the end of the sermon saying, 'The acceptable year of the Lord is Me,' and the people wanted to throw Him off a cliff. Here was Eternal Life walking the earth and people rejected it.

How to rule over depression

There are more people committing suicide right now than there have ever been in the history of mankind. There is depression all around us. We hear of people committing suicide, people being killed in plane crashes, one war stopping and another starting.

Depression is an emotional problem. Human emotion is a soulish action of the adamic or the sinful nature. It has nothing to do with your spirit man once you are recreated. This is where many people get confused. They talk about inner healing, trying to find out what is inside their spirit. Inside your spirit if you are born again, you have the Trinity. The Bible says you are born of the incorruptible seed, which is the Word of God. The Bible says that you are a new creature: all old things are passed away.

We need to deal with the soul and the physical body – this is where we have problems as Christians. We have been recreated, we are spirit beings born again of Jesus Christ. The problem if you are born again (and even more so if you are filled with the Spirit of God) is not with your spirit – it is with your soulish realm because your physical body and your soulish realm are not born again when you are. *You are a spirit* and that is what is born again. If you have false teeth for instance, when you get born again, you will still have false teeth afterwards.

In these last days the key to walking in victory is knowing you are a spirit and letting your spirit dominate and be victorious over your five senses. We don't have to take what the world offers, we don't have to live as the world lives. We are 'super human beings', *in* this world but not *of* this world (John 17.16). You need to understand who you are in Christ when you are born again. You become a brand new creature and the God that created the universe comes and lives inside you and that is why all things are possible to you. How many of you would like to have done what John the Baptist did? He was a great preacher anointed of God yet the Bible says, 'The least in the kingdom of God is greater than John the Baptist.' Hallelujah!

Let us look at some of the symptoms of depression. Firstly, becoming a recluse – being withdrawn from reality. Many people think that if they can withdraw from reality they have the answer and that is why drugs and alcohol have such an effect on the world today. Mike Warnke was a drug addict who found Jesus as his Saviour and has a tremendous testimony. One story he tells is this. He took drugs to get 'out of it' and one day he woke up to find the refrigerator empty so he thought, 'Well, I am just going to get right out of it again.' He took more drugs and when he woke the second time his refrigerator was gone!

All drugs do is worsen the situation. People have to take more and more and it becomes a continuous cycle of taking drugs. Eventually the devil will kill him. He steals, kills and destroys. Actually he doesn't have to kill them, he just lets them kill themselves.

A passive mind is another symptom of depression. The values of life just don't matter. One of the things about the hippy movement was that they claimed to have all the answers – they claimed to know exactly how it all worked out and yet they had to take LSD to make it work. Now if someone has the answer, surely they don't have to take something that will destroy their brain to make it work for them.

We have the Spirit of God in us and He is consistent. We don't have hangovers or a 'high' or 'low'.

Another reason for depression is magnifying difficulties. Have you ever noticed that all the difficulties of this earth are headlines on the front page of the newspapers and all the victories are in small print on the back page? Everybody always talks about the difficulties but what is the point of talking about them unless you have the solution? Don't talk about the problems, talk about the solutions. That is what Jesus did. He said, 'I am the truth, the way and the life.'

Another symptom is lack of ambition and activity. The Bible tells us that without a vision God's people will perish. One of the thoughts that keeps the world going is that tomorrow will be better than today. Everybody has a vision or a dream that one day things will be better than they are now. This is a spiritual principle. If you have no hope then you have nothing to put your faith to. Once you have hope you can take your faith and apply it to the hope, then your faith will work for you. Faith is the substance of things hoped for and if you have no hope you cannot apply your faith to anything – you will be like a motorcar running in neutral. That is why the Bible says you will perish without a vision. You should dream big dreams for God, have a vision for your children and begin to take that hope and raise it up and then apply faith to it.

Let us examine some of the causes of depression.

One of the greatest causes of depression is *disappointment*, and do you know why people get disappointed? Because they have their faith in man instead of in God. If your faith is in a church or the preacher, then you will be disappointed. Jesus Christ is the Head of the Church and your faith should be in Him. When our faith is in people and they let us down, we can become depressed, disillusioned and confused. Then we have a pity party! But you are in charge of your destiny, you are in charge of your circumstances. Your circumstances should not rule you, you should rule them. If your circumstances are not right, change them according to the Word of God through Jesus Christ. Circumstances are subject to change.

Failure is another reason why people are walking about depressed. The reason why so many people fail in the world today is because the world system is designed for you to fail. All you hear is how much you can borrow, how much you can get – your house, your aeroplane, your fishing rod, your swimming pool, whatever it is – all you have to do is borrow. But no one talks about the fact that you have to pay it back with interest added on. The world system is not there for your benefit. As a matter of fact, there are about two hundred people on this earth today who control the whole economy, the fuel and the food, and all they do is have a little war down the road when things are not going their way and change everything about. But God's system is not dependent on the economy. His system is not dependent on the stock market. God, who created this world, is our source *not* the world system, and God wants to give you all that you need.

Another reason for depression is *religion that is dead or cultish.* Tradition and religion have taught us that the poorer you are, the more spiritual you are and the devil has given us that lie because *without any finance, we cannot reach the world for Jesus.* Without any finance, we cannot reach Africa for Jesus. Before you can bless anybody you have to be blessed. We want to go into Africa and give the people food and clothes as well as preaching deliverance and the healing power of Jesus, and we need finances to do that.

If people are in a church where death is being preached, that is exactly what they will be – dead. If you attend a church where you fall asleep time after time and all the preacher talks about is sin and death, it will make you depressed. You will walk out feeling worse than when you went in.

Depression is also caused by natural disasters, the loss of a loved one, a job or a business, and unfortunately, many people think that God is responsible. Their attitude is, 'Oh, well, if God is doing it, I will just have to accept it.' If you lose your job through the devil, then all you do is believe that God will give you a better one.

Many people say that God is giving people terminal diseases, yet someone who believes that it is God's will for them to have cancer will do everything to get better and go against the will of God! It is not a blessing for you to be sick. Not even the people in the world can be convinced that sickness is better than health, it is only the church who will believe that it is God's will for them to be sick and that it is more of a blessing than being healthy.

We should look to Jesus as the author and developer of our faith – not aunty, uncle, the Sunday School teacher, or anyone else except Jesus. My faith is in Jesus and Jesus tells me that He took my sickness so I don't have to be sick any more.

How to deal with depression

1. The most important thing that you must realise is that you can't rule over depression yourself. There is a foolish doctrine called Humanism that says you are God and you control your destiny, you are the one who takes the place of God and what you do is up to you. I have met some of the wealthiest people on this earth and some of the greatest sportsmen and not one of them has the key to ruling over depression and oppression and the fear in their lives unless they know Jesus.

I was called out urgently one night to visit a very successful woman. When we arrived, she was in bed having taken about thirty pills. She said that she could not take the pressures of life any more.

The Bible gives us the key to ruling in life.

> But seek ye first the kingdom of God, and his righteousness; and all these things shall be added unto you (Matt. 6.33).

The Bible does not say you can do all things, it says you can do all things *through Christ Jesus*. You are a failure without Jesus Christ as the source of your life.

> For the kingdom of God is not meat and drink; but righteousness, and peace, and joy in the Holy Ghost (Rom. 14.17).

The Holy Ghost will give you peace and joy.

2. You must know the dominion and authority of the believer. To rule in life you have to know who you are in Christ Jesus. Most people don't know the Word of God and so they don't know what they have. Some people know their insurance policy better than they know the Word of God. Most people know the laws of the land. If someone walks in and tries to take things out of their house, they would call the police. Yet when the devil is stealing from them, they don't know what God's Word says about it and so he robs them of everything and they just accept it thinking that God is trying to teach them something.

Jesus said that the devil comes to steal, kill and destroy, not God. Our insurance policy is the New Testament. It tells us that Jesus came to give us abundant life *but we have to enforce it.* We have been given the authority – the Bible tells us:

> Verily I say unto you, Whatsoever ye shall bind on earth shall be bound in heaven: and whatsoever ye shall loose on earth shall be loosed in heaven (Matt. 18.18).

You have the authority and dominion on this earth so bind the devil in your life. A traffic policeman does not stop a ten ton truck physically, but when he is wearing his uniform and whistle all he has to do is lift his hand and the truck will stop. God gave me this illustration. He said that most Christians are going out naked, without a uniform, which is the armour of God, the breastplate of righteousness. All they really have is the helmet of salvation, their feet are not even shod with the gospel of peace and they have no shield of faith or sword of the Spirit – they are naked. Imagine the peak hour traffic at five p.m. and someone from the Traffic Department comes along wearing just his little hat – he would not last long! The Lord said to me, 'If you will walk around wearing your full uniform, you can stand up in the middle of the street and in the spirit realm those demons will come running at you at a hundred miles an hour. All you need say is, "Stop, in Jesus' name," and they will stop dead in their tracks because you have the authority.' He said, 'You will say, "Devil go, in Jesus' name," and he will have to go because you have the authority.'

> Now thanks be unto God, which always causeth us to triumph in Christ, and maketh manifest the savour of his knowledge by us in every place (2 Cor. 2.14). (Always, not one out of ten).

'All power is given unto me in heaven and in the earth, now you go....' Jesus did not say that all power was given unto the devil but we should just hang on till one day we cross the river in the sweet by and by. If Jesus has *all* the power then the devil cannot have any.

You need to let the Spirit of God work in you and He will do exceeding abundantly above all that you can even ask or think. You need to meditate on that. Everything you ask, everything you have thought, He is able to do exceeding abundantly above all. Hallelujah! How can you be depressed as a Christian? When depression comes along, you say, 'Depression, leave, I am a child of God, I don't know you.'

That is why we have to lead a spirit dominated life. The Bible tells us in Galatians chapter 5 that when we walk in the Spirit we will not fulfil the lust of the flesh. When you let your spirit man dominate your five physical senses you will get in line with the Word of God and you will only think on things that are pure, honest and of good report. You will not think of things in the world.

The Bible tells me whatever I put my hands to will prosper, that the angels are encamped around about me to protect me, that I am an overcomer because I am born of God and whatsoever is born of God overcometh this world. I walk by faith and not by sight, I am a child of God and the devil has to leave.

The devil is after the mind. That is the battleground. He

cannot touch the spirit but he tries to attack the mind. Jesus said that the devil has only delegated power and authority so whatever you allow him to have is what he will have.

Jesus ruled over depression by always asserting a spirit of dominion. He never made a negative confession. When He prayed, He said, 'Father, I thank you that you have heard me, but I am just saying this so that these people with unbelief can hear what I am doing' (John 11.41–42 – paraphrased). When the devil attacked Him in the wilderness He did not say, 'God, I am your son, don't you know what is going on here?' No, He simply said, 'It is written.' He took the sword of the Spirit, the Word of God, and defeated the devil.

Jesus understood His relationship with the Father. We need to understand the character of God and also the Father/son relationship. Even the best father/son relationship on this earth cannot compare with the relationship between our Father God and His children. The battle has been won, we just need to enforce it.

2. The mind

One of the major areas where Christians are attacked by Satan is through the mind. For a few weeks after being born again and Spirit filled, they float on a cloud; then gradually doubt and fear begin to creep in.

When you are born again neither your mind nor your body is reborn but only your spirit man. *It is up to you to renew your mind* and to gain victory over the devil in the mental realm.

> Wherefore gird up the loins of your mind, be sober, and hope to the end for the grace that is to be brought unto you at the revelation of Jesus Christ (1 Pet. 1.13).

> Let this mind be in you, which was also in Christ Jesus (Phil. 2.5).

...But we have the mind of Christ (l Cor. 2.16).

When you are born again, you receive Jesus into your heart or spirit man, so as this is where the mind of Christ lives, it is up to you to let the mind of Christ run its full course through your mind. This is the key.

A spiritual giant is someone who thinks in line with his spirit man. If the devil can get you to act on the thoughts he puts into your mind, he will have you defeated in every area. While you live on this earth in a body that is not yet glorified, the devil will attack your five physical senses because he is the god of this world and therefore has the right to attack you in the sense realm. It is *your* responsibility to defeat Satan in this realm on the earth. The mind suffers great onslaughts through the power of darkness and God desires the human mind to be under divine subjection so it must be directed through the human spirit by the Holy Spirit.

Many people cannot understand how their loved ones can see the change in their lives and yet still not accept what they say. This is an example of how Satan can rule the mind.

In whom the god of this world hath blinded the minds of them which believe not, lest the light of the glorious gospel of Christ, who is the image of God, should shine unto them (2 Cor. 4.4).

God cannot be the god of this world blinding their minds so that they will not believe. He is talking about Satan being the god of this world. We should pray that Satan loose their minds from the power of darkness so that when somebody does minister to them they will be open to receive.

There is a story of a missionary who was taken prisoner in Vietnam. He noticed an eagle sitting on a table very tamely and before they left camp the next morning, he went over to the bird and saw that its eyes were stitched closed. When he asked why they would do such a terrible thing, they said that the bird would not stay there for a second if its eyes were open, but when the eyes are shut, it has no fear or awareness of reality. So the bird will just stay there because it thinks that it is safe. It is the same with many human beings – because they are blinded from the light of the gospel of Jesus, they think they are safe.

Another area over which Satan rules is a *reprobate mind*. Romans 1. 18–22 explains why people now worship reptiles, birds and other creatures instead of worshipping the living God.

> For the wrath of God is revealed from heaven against all ungodliness and unrighteousness of men, who hold the truth in unrighteousness: because that which may be known of God is manifest in them; for God hath shewed it unto them. [How does He show Himself to us?] For the invisible things of him from the creation of the world are clearly seen, being understood by the things that are made, even his eternal power and Godhead; so that they are without excuse: Because that, when they knew God, they glorified him not as God, neither were thankful; but became vain in their imaginations, and their foolish heart was darkened. Professing themselves to be wise, they became fools.

Without God in your life you are a fool. People say that it is education that keeps them away from God but it is their *lack* of it. If you think that you can take the place of God or have your own salvation by believing in yourself, it is foolish thinking.

> And changed the glory of uncorruptible God into an image made like to corruptible man, and to birds, and four footed beasts, and creeping things (Rom. 1.23).

The people who believe in these things have turned their backs on the living God.

The Spirit of God spoke to a woman who was a missionary in China and told her to go to a certain place and minister to the people. She told the people at the mission and they said that there was no way of getting there and that if she insisted on going they would not assist her in any way. After six days of walking, she came to the outskirts of a village and a Chinese man came out praising God. He said that he was a medical doctor and had found Jesus Christ as his Lord and Saviour and that the Lord had told him that she was coming and that he was to go with her. After the eleventh day, they had run out of water and food and they got down on their knees and prayed. While they were praying a monk appeared out of nowhere and told them to follow him. Normally the monk would not speak to a woman. They followed him and eventually came out at a monastery. There were 300 monks on their knees praising a god of some sort. They were taken to the head monk who said that three years previously, one of the monks had gone into the village and when he returned, he had a piece of torn paper which read, 'For God so loved the world that he gave his only begotten Son.' For three years they had been praying for someone to come and tell them about this God.

If you really want to know the truth, God will find a way to reveal it to you.

> And likewise, also the men, leaving the natural use of the woman, burned in their lust one toward another; men with men working that which is unseemly, and receiving in themselves that recompense of their error which was meet. And even as they did not like to retain God in their knowledge, God gave them over to a reprobate mind, to do those things which are not convenient (Rom. 1.27–8).

God is not the one who gives a person a reprobate mind, but God will allow you to do whatever you want to do. Your will is sovereign and if you want to live in sin, He will not stop you. Years ago if a child was born out of wedlock, people disapproved but today it is accepted. When I was in California, there was great excitement because it had been made legal for lesbians to take custody of children. Everybody thought it was a wonderful advance – that is a reprobate mind.

There is also the vanity of the mind, which is an *empty mind*. We find an example in Ephesians 4.17–19:

> This I say therefore, and testify in the Lord, that ye henceforth walk not as other Gentiles walk, in the vanity of their mind, having the understanding darkened, being alienated from the life of God through the ignorance that is in them, because of the blindness of their heart: Who being past feeling have given themselves over unto lasciviousness, to work all uncleanness with greediness.

We then have the fleshly mind explained in Colossians 2.18:

> Let no man beguile you of your reward in a voluntary humility and worshipping of angels, intruding into those things which he hath not seen, vainly puffed up by his fleshly mind.

Then there is the defiled mind. Titus 1.15 says:

> Unto the pure all things are pure: but unto them that are defiled and unbelieving is nothing pure; but even their mind and conscience is defiled.

The carnal mind is spoken about in Romans 8. This is the problem with most Christians – they are born again but they are living as carnal Christians, they are living like the world, as mere men as Paul says.

> For they that are after the flesh do mind the things of the flesh; but they that are after the Spirit, the things of the Spirit (Rom. 8.5).

The Bible tells us that if you walk in the spirit, you will not fulfil the lusts of the flesh.

For to be carnally minded is death (Rom. 8.6).

God is not someone who does not want you to have a good time – He is the source of abundant life. But the result of sin is death and so He is only trying to protect you. To be carnally minded is death. To walk and be controlled by the devil is death. Satan will put a carrot in front of you and dangle it twenty-four hours a day, and as you think you have got out of one mess you will be in another, and as you get out of that one, you will be deeper into another, and *eventually it will kill you*. To be carnally minded is enmity against God, the natural mind will never be in line with God's Word. The Word says we should give and it shall be given to us. The carnal mind tells you to store it up and then you will have it. The spiritual mind cannot understand that. The carnal mind says we should hate ourselves, that we are just no-good has-beens, but the spiritual mind tells us that Jesus came and died for us, that is how valuable and precious we are to God. You are somebody because Jesus lives in you. God sent His Son so that we could find the way to Him and now He is sending us so that others can find the way to Him. You are not a nobody, *you are a child of God* if you are born again.

Then there is the *unrelaxed mind* – insomnia and sleepless nights. The devil will try to attack people in that area.

When thou liest down, thou shalt not be afraid: yea, thou shalt lie down, and thy sleep shall be sweet (Prov. 3.24).

I have sweet sleep because I don't fear anything (I am not talking about reverential fear but the spirit of fear). I don't fear anything because I cast all my cares on Jesus and if He has them, I haven't and therefore I can sleep. God never slumbers or sleeps so what is the point of both of us staying up all night?

How do we have the victory over our mind in these areas? Firstly, if your thoughts do not line up with the Word of

God, cast them down to the obedience of Christ. As long as you are on this earth, the devil has an opportunity to try to put thoughts into your head. You will never get to a place where he cannot.

> For though we walk in the flesh, we do not war after the flesh; (For the weapons of our warfare are not carnal...) (2 Cor. 10.3–4).

The devil uses carnal weapons. He attacks us through our five physical senses but we are told that our weapons are spiritual. We have a sword which is the Word of God, a shield of faith, shoes shod with the gospel of peace and a helmet of salvation. We are not bound to the natural world, we have weapons that are spiritual. We have the name of Jesus.

> For the weapons of our warfare are not carnal, but mighty through God to the pulling down of strongholds (2 Cor. 10.4).

A stronghold is something that has a strong hold on your mind. 'Casting down imaginations...' Images, pictures – Satan does not defeat you with what you see with your eyes. *He defeats* you with what you see in your head. An example of this is the story of the man who had a puncture and no jack, so he decided to go to John Smith's house up the road to borrow one. On the way there the devil said to him, 'It is the middle of the night, he won't be awake.' He went a bit further, 'As a matter of fact he doesn't even like you and when you wake him up he will hate you.' Eventually he reached the front door and when John Smith answered, he said, 'I don't want your jack anyway. Who wants any help from you?' That is what the devil does. He paints images of people fighting you, talking against you, and when you receive the thoughts he has defeated you.

> Casting down imaginations and every high thing that exalteth

> itself against the knowledge of God, and bringing into captivity every thought to the obedience of Christ (2 Cor. 10.5).

If it is against God's Word, cast it down. The biggest problem we have comes when we don't replace those thoughts with the Word once they have been cast down. The Lord said that when a person gets delivered of a demon, seven more will come back if that person allows them to. Those vain imaginations will come back and test you to see whether they can stay.

> Finally, brethren, whatsoever things are true, whatsoever things are honest, whatsoever things are just, whatsoever things are pure, whatsoever things are lovely, whatsoever things are of good report; if there be any virtue, and if there be any praise, think on these things (Phil. 4.8).

God says we should think on things that are honest – the devil says we should think on things that are dishonest. God says think on things that are true – the devil says things that are untrue. Pure – impure, just – unjust, lovely – hateful. Think on these things. *The choice is yours*.

> And be not conformed to this world; but be ye transformed by the renewing of your mind, that ye may prove what is that good, and acceptable, and perfect, will of God (Rom. 12.2).

It is up to you, you are going to have to renew your mind, it is not born again when you are saved.

> Trust in the Lord with all thine heart and lean not unto thine own understanding (Prov. 3.5).

There is always a condition that goes with peace, rest and well being, and that is trust. It is the key to everything else. If you will trust in the Lord, all those things will be manifested. There is no way you can put your trust in people and have the peace of God manifest. You cannot lean to your own understanding which is carnal. 'In my opinion' or 'This is what I believe' will not get you to heaven, only the Word will get you to heaven.

> Thou wilt keep him in perfect peace, whose mind is stayed on thee: because he trusteth in thee (Isa. 26.3).

Most people have never experienced perfect peace. The Bible is not talking about keeping your mind on what God looks like but keeping your mind on the Word of God. Then you will walk in perfect peace because as soon as anything comes into your mind that is not consistent with the Word of God, you will automatically cast it down and fill your mind with the Word of God. Once it is filled it gets in line with your spirit and when mind, body and spirit are all in line with the Word of God, you have perfect peace. Jesus said:

> Therefore take no thought, saying, What shall we eat? or, What shall we drink? or, Wherewithal shall we be clothed? (Matt. 6.31).

That is how the devil gets us into defeat and this is how we can get out of it, *God's way*. A thought comes and if you meditate on that thought long enough, guess what you will do next? You will believe it, and once you believe it, guess what the next step is? You will say it, and then you have it. It works the same way for the positive. If you will meditate on God's Word long enough it will become revelation knowledge and you will believe it in your heart and say it with your mouth and when you say it, you take it. It will become part of your life. I could no more say that God made me sick than stand up and curse Him. I know the truth, it is part of me, I believe it and I say it with my mouth – I have taken that thought. If you are believing God for healing you have to get to the place where you meditate so much on healing scriptures that no thought that comes against it will have a chance to grow. You have to see yourself healed, well, and walking in health, because if you meditate on the negative side of it, that is what you will get. If you see yourself going insolvent or failing, look to the Word; it will tell you that you are more than a conqueror.

James says that a man sees himself in the Word of God, takes his face away from the mirror of the Word of God, walks away and immediately forgets what manner of man he is. A person may sit in a Sunday service and say, 'The Lord is my Shepherd, I shall not want, I know that mercy and goodness follow me.' It is in the Word of God – he sees himself in the Word of God, but by Monday he has forgotten what manner of man he is and when the devil comes to tell him that he will never amount to anything, that his business will fail, that he has no education, and will not be able to do what God wants him to do, he takes it. The Word says whatever you put your hands to will prosper. This is how the devil tried to attack Jesus, saying, 'If you are the Son of God....' There was no doubt about it, he heard God Himself say so when Jesus was baptised by John the Baptist.

> And Jesus being full of the Holy Ghost returned from Jordan... (Luke 4.1).

Jesus acted in the office of a prophet, not as the Son of God on earth. He was filled with the Holy Ghost. Jesus was a hundred per cent God and a hundred per cent man but He operated on this earth as a prophet not as God.

> And was led by the Spirit into the wilderness, being forty days tempted of the devil. And in those days he did eat nothing: and when they were ended, he afterward hungered. And the devil said unto him, If thou be the Son of God, command this stone that it be made bread (Luke 4. 1–3).

Jesus *did not say*: 'Here is my book of life, here is my passport. Look I am the Son of God, you have no right to attack me mentally, you have no right to come against me.' That is how some of us have been, 'God, help me.' God didn't say he would help – He said, 'Resist the devil in the name of Jesus and he will flee from you.' *God did everything He could nearly two thousand years ago.* If Jesus had to resist Satan, so will you.

> And Jesus answered him, saying, It is written... (Luke 4.4).

You need to know what is written before you can say that. People misconstrue the scriptures. They say, for example, 'Money is the root of all evil; godliness is next to cleanliness.' Where is that in the Bible? The devil is a legalist, he will not listen to that.

> ...That man shall not live by bread alone, but by every Word of God.

He took the sword of the Spirit, which is the Word of God, and defeated the devil.

> And the devil said unto him, All this power will I give thee, and the glory of them; for that is delivered unto me; and to whomsoever I will I give it (Luke 4.6).

Satan is the god of this world; *he was not lying.*

> If thou therefore wilt worship me, all shall be thine. And Jesus answered... (Luke 4.7).

The Lord showed me that the devil never physically took Jesus up there, he showed Him all of it in His mind. The devil did not have the authority to take the Son of God wherever he wanted physically, so he opened His mind and showed Him everything. At that split second Jesus in His mind had an image of what the devil was telling Him, right throughout the world.

> And Jesus answered and said unto him, Get thee behind me, Satan: for it is written, Thou shalt worship the Lord thy God, and him only shalt thou serve (Luke 4.8).

> And when the devil had ended all the temptation, he departed from him for a season (Luke 4.13).

That meant he was going to come back. Every day you have to build up your faith enough to be able to resist him. We must be so full of the Word that when Satan comes and tells us that we are going to fail, we can say, 'No, the Bible says that I can do all things through Christ Jesus, it is written.'

If you have a real problem, stand in front of the mirror and speak the Word of God over yourself. Say, 'Yes, it is written, whatever I put my hand to will prosper. It is written that God is able to do exceeding abundantly above all that I ask or think.' You will find that the devil will flee and you will walk in the victory that God has given you in the Word.

3. Unbelief

We need to understand what faith is, how it works, and what it is all about before we can understand doubt and unbelief. There is a big difference between unbelief and doubt.

Jesus said, 'Have faith in God' (or have the same kind of faith that you will find in the book of Genesis right through to Revelation, or have the faith that God has, the faith that God showed Abraham).

We need to know how faith works because without faith it is impossible to please Him. You cannot be saved without faith, you cannot walk in the fullness of the righteousness of God without faith.

> For verily I say unto you, That whosoever shall say unto this mountain, Be thou removed, and be thou cast into the sea; and

> shall not doubt in his heart, but shall believe that those things which he saith shall come to pass; he shall have whatsoever he saith (Mark 11.23).

Jesus did not say that you will have whatsoever you say – He said that you will have whatsoever you believe in your heart *and* say with your mouth. That is why you don't die when you say you are dying for a cup of tea, you don't really believe it. People say, 'He tickled me to death, I'm afraid.' 'I can't come, he scared me to death.' We should speak life and say we are living to have a cup of tea! The world considers us very strange because the devil has programmed the world to death.

> Therefore I say unto you, What things soever ye desire, when ye pray… [*when you pray* not when you see it]… believe that ye receive them, and ye shall have them (Mark 11.24).

You have to believe that you receive *when you pray*. That means you cannot believe with your natural eyes – when you see it you know it. Faith is opposite to the world's way. The world says, 'When I see it, I will believe it.' That doesn't take much believing, does it? The Bible tells us that you have to believe that you have it, then – *and only then* – will you see it. That is why no amount of crying to God will change anything. It is only *faith* which will bring the manifestation of what is needed from the spiritual realm into the natural realm.

Unbelief is *refusal* to trust God's Word.

> If any of you lack wisdom, let him ask of God, that giveth to all men liberally, and upbraideth not; and it shall be given him. But let him ask in faith, nothing wavering. For he that wavereth is like a wave of the sea driven with the wind and tossed. For let not that man think that he shall receive anything of the Lord. A double minded man is unstable in all his ways (James 1.5–8).

If you are not receiving from the Lord, here is your problem. You are being double minded. Doubt means to waver in judgement, to hesitate in indecision. Most Christians are not walking in unbelief, but in doubt. People say, 'I believe that the Word of God says this but just in case it doesn't work, I will do this.' Doubt comes in, you become double minded, you take one step forward and one step back and eventually you will fall.

Unbelief is a negative and unreasonable action. Unbelief does not believe at all. A doubter will say, 'I believe in the Holy Ghost and I would like to be filled with the evidence of speaking in other tongues, but I have tried four or five times and it is not working for me.' Or 'I know that tongues is for today because I have seen others speaking in tongues but nothing has happened for me.' That is being double minded.

> Take heed, brethren, lest there be in any of you an evil heart of unbelief, in departing from the living God (Heb. 3.12).

Unbelief is a satanic force. For example, someone will say 'I believe that speaking in tongues is of the devil.' That is refusing God's Word, not doubting it. There are many people in unbelief because they do not believe the Word of God. We have theologians saying that angels do not exist but Jesus Himself told us how the angels came and fed Him and ministered to Him and Psalm 91 speaks of angels. It is in God's Word.

People say that they have gone beyond the Bible and found out that there is no devil! According to them, Jesus must have imagined strange things when He came out of the wilderness, and He could not have meant it when He said that we should cast out devils. But the Word of God says that the devil tempted Jesus in the wilderness and Jesus told us that we would cast out devils in His name.

Jesus Christ never came to this earth to prove that He was the Son of God. He came to meet the needs of the people. There are people today who are sick, full of drugs, oppressed and depressed and Jesus is the same today as He was then. He loves them just as much now as He did when He died for them. Healing can never pass away because there are people who are sick, and Jesus said, 'I have come for the sick.' We are called believers and yet we have unbelief in certain areas. How can we be *unbelieving believers?* Unbelief screamed, 'If thou be the Son of God, come down from the cross,' rather than seeking the purpose of Christ dying on the cross. Unbelief denies the deity and lordship of Christ. Unbelief cried, 'These men are full of new wine,' without finding out whether it was a gift from God.

> And I say unto you, Ask, and it shall be given you; seek, and ye shall find; knock, and it shall be opened unto you. [Jesus will not break the door down.] For every one that asketh receiveth; and he that seeketh findeth; and to him that knocketh it shall be opened. If a son shall ask bread of any of you that is a father, will he give him a stone? Or if he ask a fish, will he for a fish give him a serpent? (Luke 11.9–11).

I have seen people who don't want to ask God for the Holy Spirit in case they get something else. Whatever you ask God for in the name of Jesus, He will give you as long as it is in line with His Word. If you ask amiss, the devil will make sure he gives it to you.

> Or if he shall ask an egg, will he offer him a scorpion? (Luke 11.12).

This is the way many people think of God – 'Maybe God gave me this sickness to teach me something.' He never did – He will give you what you ask for but you have got to be single minded.

> If ye then, being evil, know how to give good gifts unto your

children; how much more shall your heavenly Father give the Holy Spirit to them that ask him? (Luke 11.13).

There are many people who say that the evidence of speaking in other tongues is given by the devil. Do they think that God and the devil are working together, that when they ask God the Father for the Holy Ghost the devil comes to give it to them? The devil is against speaking in tongues because he does not know what you are saying to your Father – it is your supernatural communication with your Father and he cannot understand what you are saying. The whole New Testament was written by tongue-talkers. That's a good sign!

Unbelief cried to Jesus who was praying for the sick, 'You are the prince of devils.' That is what they said to Jesus without seeking to know the truth and Jesus said, 'A house divided against itself will not stand.' If God is putting the sickness on you and also taking it off, then His house is divided against Himself. If the devil is casting out devils, he will not stand, he is divided, he is defeating himself. The devil has divided the Church and we have become double minded. If I said that God will heal some people and not others while I was praying for the sick, who would know if it was God's will for them? If I said that God had shown me that it is only His will for ten per cent to be saved, then everybody would sit and say, 'I wonder if it is His will for me to be saved or not?' – and nobody would receive salvation.

Your faith begins where the will of God is known. The problem with most people is that they have not found out the will of God for their life and therefore cannot apply faith to it. When you know that God has called you to the ministry then you can apply your faith to the situation. When you know that God has placed you in a business and that it is God's will you can apply your faith to that business. But a lot of people are trying to apply their faith to something that is not God's will, and they cannot understand why it is not working.

Someone says, 'But didn't you say that you can have whatsoever you desire?' Yes, but the Bible also says 'Delight yourself in the Lord and he will give you the desires of your heart' (Psalm 37.4). He is the One who will put the desires into your heart.

No spiritual thing can flourish in an atmosphere of unbelief. Unbelief demands statistics and material evidence rather than faith. It caused Israel to wander in the wilderness for forty years.

> And Moses verily was faithful in all his house, as a servant, for a testimony of those things which were to be spoken after; But Christ as a son over his own house; whose house are we, if we hold fast the confidence and the rejoicing of the hope firm unto the end (Heb. 3.5–6).

Hope is scriptural and has its place. My hope is in the coming of the Lord Jesus. It is not my faith in the coming of the Lord Jesus because He is going to come whether I have faith in it or not. Your faith is not going to determine whether Jesus comes, He is coming whether you believe it or not; just as you will never die, you are a spirit and you are either going to hell or to heaven, *whether you believe it or not*. Whether or not you believe the law of gravity, you will find out it works if you throw yourself off a three storey building!

Hope is what you put your faith to. If you have no hope you have no vision, you have no dream, you have nothing to put your faith to. It is like a car running in neutral. Let me give you an example. God showed me the calling that I had in my ministry. He showed me what He wanted me to do and hope arose in my heart. I began to visualise this ministry even further into the future than it is now. I then took my faith and put it to the hope. Hope has its place but it is not faith. *Most people are living in hope instead of faith.*

When we were in America, we were believing God for certain finances to start our ministry here. One night I was lying on the bed and the Spirit of the Lord said to me, 'How would you really react if you had the money in your pocket?' I got off the bed and began to dance around the room. Although my pockets were empty, my faith said that I had it and I had to act that way.

Too many people confess out of fear. I have had someone say to me, 'My, you look sick,' and my first reaction has been, 'By His stripes I was healed, He took my infirmities, He bore my sicknesses, I am prosperous....' I wanted to get into the whole Word, and the Lord said, 'What do you really believe?' I said, 'That I am healed,' and He said, 'Well, then, just keep quiet – you don't have to convince me that you are healed.' If you really are in faith you will act as though you have received it because you will know that in the spiritual realm you have it and all you are doing is waiting for it to manifest in the physical realm. You may have nothing in your pocket but you must walk down the street as if you are the most prosperous person in that street.

> Harden not your hearts, as in the provocation, in the day of temptation in the wilderness: When your fathers tempted me, proved me, and saw my works forty years. Wherefore I was grieved with that generation, and said, They do alway err in their heart; and they have not known my ways. So I sware in my wrath, They shall not enter into my rest. Take heed, brethren, lest there be in any of you an evil heart of unbelief, in departing from the living God. But exhort one another daily, while it is called Today; lest any of you be hardened through the deceitfulness of sin. For we are made partakers of Christ, if we hold the beginning of our confidence steadfast unto the end; While it is said, Today if ye will hear his voice, harden not your hearts, as in the provocation. For some, when they had heart, did provoke: howbeit not all that came out of Egypt by Moses. But with whom was he grieved forty years? was it not with them that had sinned, whose carcases fell in the wilderness? And to whom sware he that they should not enter into his rest, but to them that believed not? So we see that they could not enter in because of unbelief.

> Let us therefore fear, lest, a promise being left us of entering into his rest, any of you should seem to come short of it. For unto us was the gospel preached, as well as unto them: but the word preached did not profit them: not being mixed with faith in them that heard it (Heb. 3.8–4.2).

You can hear scriptures of healing, deliverance and salvation from the Word of God but *if you do not mix them with faith*, they will not help you at all.

'Now faith is the substance of things hoped for...' [You have to put your faith to the things you hope for to bring them into natural manifestation of material substance] '... the evidence of things not seen' (Heb. 11.1).

The Lord will tell you just a little bit at a time because you need to walk by faith continuously. If you reached the place where you knew exactly what was going to happen, there would be no need to exercise your faith because it is the evidence of things not seen. We must know God's Word and spend time in it because His Word and His will are one and your faith begins where the will of God is known. If you don't know God's Word you cannot apply faith to it. If I say that I don't think God will heal anybody here, He might if He wants to, but I don't think so, you will have no hope. What I need to do is share the Word of God because hope and faith come by hearing. When I say, 'By his stripes you were healed,' hope will come, because you will see that God wants you to be healed. Then you can take your faith and apply it to your hope and because faith is the evidence of things not seen, you will receive the manifestation. *People don't get healed in some churches for the simple reason that they don't preach healing.* God confirms His Word, the gospel, the good news.

> For God sent not his Son into the world to condemn the world, but that the world through him might be saved (John 3.17).

You can have all the money you like but if you have cancer you are not prosperous. The greatest and most prosperous thing that exists is being born again, having the life of God dwelling in you. You must act on the Word of God to get rid of doubt and unbelief. You are the establishing witness in everything when it comes to God's Word and the devil and his lies – you are in the middle. Either you go with God and His Word or you go with the devil and his lies.

> But be ye doers of the Word, and not hearers only, deceiving your own selves. For if any be a hearer of the Word, and not a doer, he is like unto a man beholding his natural face in a glass. [The Word of God is the glass or mirror.] For he beholdeth himself, and goeth his way, and straightway forgetteth what manner of man he was (Jas. 1.22–4).

James is saying that you read in your Bible that you are more than a conqueror through Christ Jesus, that God shall supply all your need according to His riches in glory by Christ Jesus. You see yourself in the Word of God as the Word tells you. Jesus became sin who knew no sin that you might be made the righteousness of God. So you see yourself as righteous. You then put your Bible down and go away and forget what manner of person you are and what the Word says about you and you will get right into the devil's grasp. He will say that you are not righteous. Do you know why? Because you do not act on what you are in the Word. You are an ambassador for Jesus; act like it.

> But whoso looketh into the perfect law of liberty, and continueth therein, he being not a forgetful hearer, but a doer of the work, this man shall be blessed in his deed (Jas. 1.25).

You have to *act* on the Word of God – Noah, Moses, Joseph, Peter, Paul – all received the blessings of God. Have you ever thought about Noah? He acted on the Word and built an ark when they had never seen rain. He had people asking what it was for and when he told them it was for the rain, they said, 'Rain? What is that?' But when you go with God's Word and act on it, no matter what people say, *you will never drown.*

4. Fear

There has never been more fear on the earth than there is today. I have never seen so much propaganda going out to cause people to walk in fear. We have been conditioned to fear. If you do not walk in fear the world thinks there is something wrong with you, and they are right, there is. You are an anointed child of God, *you are peculiar.*

Firstly, you need to realise that faith originates from God and fear originates from the devil. The devil never created anything, all he did was pervert faith. I am not talking about the reverential fear that we have in God, that is respect for God. The Bible tells us to fear the Lord, meaning reverencing God, but I am talking about human fear that was perverted from faith to fear by the enemy. Genesis 3.10 proves this. The first account of fear found in the Bible is when Adam said 'I heard your voice and I was afraid.' While Adam was walking in fellowship with God he walked in faith, but when he sinned fear came. Fear did not exist before sin came and for the first time Adam said he was afraid.

Human fear has been called man's deadliest enemy. Doctors have a list of over forty modern fears people suffer from: cats, dogs, mice, heights, etc. It is a shame that most Christians are included in the world when it comes to fear. The Bible says 'What is not of faith is sin' in Romans 14, therefore fear in a child of God is sin. I will show you why you shouldn't fear.

> For God hath not given us the spirit of fear (2 Tim. 1.7).

Well, if God hasn't given it to you, what are you doing

with it? When the devil knocks on the door, don't sign for the package of fear. Fear is a spirit – when the wealthiest man on earth won't come out of his house for fear of catching germs that will kill him, that is a spirit. When people won't come out of their house for fear of things around them, that is a spirit. When someone won't go into an elevator because they have a fear that it will not get them to the next floor, that is a spirit. *If allowed to, that spirit will get you to a place where it will destroy and kill you.*

The Bible says: 'For God hath not given us the spirit of fear, but of power, and of love, and of a sound mind.' You have the right, through what Jesus did on the cross for you in the plan of redemption, to walk in love, power and have a sound mind.

> My people are destroyed for lack of knowledge (Hos. 4.6).

As from now you will never have to fear again as long as you live. God said in His Word 366 times 'Fear not'. I believe He knew *what He meant* and I believe *He meant what he said.* You have been given enough scriptures telling you to 'Fear not'.

Faith heals, sets free, receives from God and walks in liberty. Fear confuses your mind, consumes energy, creates terror. We are told in 1 John 4.18 that fear has torment. That spirit will torment you, it will create terror, it will hinder your walk with God and make you mentally and physically ill.

The first kind of fear that a Christian lives with is *failure*.

The world conditions you to fail, the devil doesn't like to see winners. There are so many negative things going around this earth right now trying to get us to fail, but *we don't fail*, we play until we win. It is our bat and our ball and God is the umpire! All we do is get up off the ground and go on until we win. We might have the opportunity to fail, but we don't because we can do all things through Christ Jesus who strengthens us – greater is He that is in us than he that is in the world.

> Now [not in the sweet by and by, not in the past], thanks be unto God, which always causeth us to triumph in Christ (2 Cor. 2.14).

It doesn't matter what the situation looks like, we know the end result. I do not fear to fail because I have the mind of Christ, because God has given me a spirit of wisdom and revelation in the knowledge of Him, because I have the name of Jesus.

Secondly, most Christians have a fear of *responsibility*.

How can you say that you are not capable of doing the work of the ministry? How can you say you are not capable of praying for someone who is sick? How can you say that you are not capable of succeeding in your business when you have the God that created the universe, the God that said 'Light be' and light was, living in you? I said to Jim Spillman one say 'How are you?'

He replied 'How am I? I have the God who created the universe living in me, how can I be? Blessed with all spiritual blessings, more than a conqueror through Christ Jesus. If God be for me who can be against me?'

Nothing is impossible to him who believes. You need to have the revelation of the 'new creation'.

John the Baptist was an anointed prophet of God who shook Israel with his preaching and Jesus said, 'The least in my kingdom is greater than he.' Jesus said, 'The glory, Father, that you have given me, I now give unto them.' That is why all things are possible to us. These works shall we do and greater works. Some of you say, 'Yes, but the greater work is being born again.' That is correct, but He still said 'These works shall you do.' You should be doing the works of Jesus. You have been given the ability to do anything that God wants you to do. People ask me to pray for more power. I say you have the Father, the Son and the Holy Spirit living in you, there is no more power left. *When you call on number one and He lives in you there is no one else you can call on.*

Another fear that Christians have is their *past lives*.

The devil will always remind you of failure in your past life. The Bible tells you that if any man be in Christ he is a brand new creature, old things have passed away and everything has become new (2 Cor. 5. 17). When the devil comes to remind you of what you did in 1975, tell him that person died, he doesn't exist any more. You don't remember him, *you are a brand new creation.* When you come to Jesus He recreates you, He makes you a brand new creature, the slate is wiped clean. God doesn't just forgive, He forgets. Paul told us not to look behind us but to press on to the goal that is ahead of us, and when the devil comes to tell you that you are going to fail, say '*No* devil, this is just another opportunity to prove God is true and you are a liar. And when all this is over and I have the victory, I will stand up and tell people what a liar you are, I will tell people how we defeated you through Jesus Christ, and I will give Jesus all the glory.'

Another one is fear of the *future*.

If you don't know Jesus Christ you have a reason to fear the future. There are two definite things that I know in the future. One is that the Bible tells us that the righteous will not be forsaken and that they will not be begging bread (Ps. 37.25). So we are not going to be begging bread and we are not going to be forsaken because the Word of God tells us that He will never leave us nor forsake us. He tells us that He will meet *all* our needs – every one of them – according to His riches in glory.

The other thing that we can be sure about is that Jesus is coming back.

> Therefore I tell you, stop being perpetually uneasy (anxious and worried) about your life, what you shall eat or what you shall drink, and about your body, what you shall put on. Is not life greater (in quality) than food, and the body (far above and more excellent) than clothing? [You are created in the image of God, do you think God is just going to let born again believers – His family – perish?] Look at the birds of the air; they neither sow nor reap nor gather into barns, and yet your Heavenly Father keeps feeding them. Are you not worth more than they? And which of you by worrying and being anxious can add one unit of measure to his stature or to the span of his life? (Matt. 6.25–27, Amplified Bible).

Worrying worsens the situation, *worrying is distrust of God's Word.* It cuts off your faith which you need to communicate with God and to bring the things that you need into manifestation. The devil lies to you, he comes and tells you that you had better worry about the situation or otherwise you don't care and are not concerned about it and that means you have no interest in it and it is just going to come and overtake you.

The Bible tells us to cast our cares upon Jesus (1 Pet. 5.7). Either you have them or He has them and if He has them it means that you don't have to worry about them – Jesus will sort them out. People say 'God, I cast this care upon you,' then they get up and say 'Oh, I don't know what I am going to do,' and take the care right back.

> But seek for (aim at and strive after) first of all his Kingdom, and his righteousness (His way of doing and being right), and then all these things taken together will be given you besides. [Most people are trying to add the things before they seek Him.] So do not worry or be anxious about tomorrow, for tomorrow will have worries and anxieties of its own (Matt. 6.33, Amplified Bible).

You can't have enough faith for tomorrow, so worrying about tomorrow today will not help one bit. Worries and anxieties will be here until Jesus comes back, it is how you react to them that counts. You think that if you confess over your business ten or fifteen times everything will just straighten out, but the devil will fight you. However, you don't have to receive the worries. The devil will ask you who will look after the children? All you do is say 'My God looks after the birds, He is surely going to look after me and my family.'

Fear of *sickness and disease* is very common.

A person gets a pain in the chest and automatically thinks it is a heart attack because Aunty so-and-so died of a heart attack. A little lump is suddenly cancer. The devil is right there just waiting for you to agree with him. When he comes and tells you that the disease has been passed down through the family, say 'Yes, but which family are you talking about? I am in the family of God now, and in the family of God we walk in divine health.' Start agreeing with Jesus.

How to rule over fear

Firstly, *it is not God's will for you to fear.* God will not tell you to do something you are not capable of, and He has told you 366 times not to fear so He must know that you are capable of it.

Secondly, we must *meditate on God's Word* and not the devil's lies, because what you meditate on you will get. Don't meditate on worldly songs. They are full of 'I, I who have nothing' and 'Yesterday all my troubles seemed so far away – now they are here to stay'!! They are sure to depress you.

The divorce rate in many countries is extremely high. When you meditate on soap box operas that are full of divorce and suicide that is what you will get. TV commercials are full of 'When you get the flu', 'When your house catches fire' etc, but we don't need to listen to that. We have the Sunday Bible Times.

> Be strong and of a good courage; be not afraid, neither be thou dismayed: for the Lord thy God is with thee withersoever thou goest (Josh. 1.9).

> I will trust and not be afraid: for the Lord JEHOVAH is my strength and my song (Isa. 12.2).

> Yea, though I walk in the valley of the shadow of death, I will fear no evil (Ps. 23.4).

It does not matter what evil comes against you, you do not have to fear it. The shadow of a dog cannot bite you and only the shadow of death is what a Christian experiences – he never experiences death itself. It is a shadow because when he is absent from the body, he is present with the Lord. Hallelujah!

> Fear thou not; for I am with thee: be not dismayed; for I am thy

> God: I will strengthen thee; yea, I will help thee; yea, I will uphold thee with the right hand of my righteousness: Behold, all they that were incensed against thee shall be ashamed and confounded: they shall be as nothing; and they that strive with thee shall perish (Isa. 41.10–11).

He is talking about the devil and his demons and anybody who comes against you under their influence.

Thirdly, if you want to walk free from fear, you must *act on God's Word.*

> And why call ye me, Lord, Lord, and do not the things which I say? (Luke 6.46).

There will be many people who will face judgement one day who will say, 'But I don't understand, Lord, why have you left me out of everything?' The Lord may reply, 'Because you did not act on my Word, you just used the name of Christian.' Some people think that if they stand in church, they automatically become a Christian. How many people sleep in a garage and come out a motor car? We are talking about a personal relationship with Jesus.

> Whosoever cometh to me, and heareth my sayings, and doeth them, I will shew you to whom he is like: he is like a man which built an house, and digged deep, and laid the foundation on a rock [the rock is acting on God's Word] and when the flood arose, the stream beat vehemently upon that house, and could not shake it: for it was founded upon a rock. [Now the same man in the same situation] But he that heareth, and doeth not, is like a man that without a foundation built an house upon the earth; against which the stream did beat vehemently, and immediately it fell; and the ruin of that house was great (Luke 6.47–49).

Two people can be in the same church, saved and filled with the Spirit of God, come to the same number of services a week, but if one acts on the Word and the other does not, *the one will stand and the other will fall* when the floods of life come against them.

Lastly, we must *walk in love.*

The Lord said that the times you get out of love are the times you get into fear. As soon as you allow fear to come upon you, you get out of love.

> There is no fear in love; but perfect love casteth out fear (1 John 4.18).

When pressure comes against you and you become fearful, you begin to fight with your spouse, your children, the people employed by you, even yourself. When fear comes, perfect love goes. As soon as perfect love comes, fear goes. If you are walking in perfect love and in the Word then fear cannot come on you.

5. Anger

> Be not hasty in thy spirit to be angry: for anger resteth in the bosom of fools (Eccles. 7.9).

Anger was one of the hardest areas in my life to overcome. All the devil did was make sure that my car would not start, or that I could not find matching socks or that my eggs were too soft or too hard, and I would get angry!

> Cease from anger, and forsake wrath: fret not thyself in any wise to do evil (Ps. 37.8).

> He that is soon angry dealeth foolishly; and a man of wicked devices is hated (Prov. 14.17).

If you are not walking in the spirit the devil can make you angry any time he wants. Jesus said 'Whosoever is angry with his brother without a cause shall be in danger of the judgment' (Matt. 5.22). I asked the Lord if He meant that I could get angry if I had cause. He said, 'No, there is nothing to cause you to be angry with your brother because the royal law is to love one another.'

> Wherefore, my beloved brethren, let every man be swift to hear, slow to speak, slow to wrath (Jas. 1.19).

> A soft answer turneth away wrath: but grievous words stir up anger (Prov. 15.1).

The saying 'Sticks and stones may break my bones but words will never harm me' *is a lie from the pit of hell.* So many people will not speak to a member of their family or a good friend because of something that was said. More churches have been destroyed by the mouth than by anything else.

> Let all bitterness, and wrath, and anger, and clamour, and evil speaking, be put away from you, with all malice (Eph. 4.31).

People agree with confessions, but they only confess what suits them. 'By His stripes I am healed. My God supplies all my needs.' But when it comes to confessing good over the next door neighbour, they don't want to. God showed me that the same spiritual principles that are used in confession of God's Word over healing and prosperity must be used when it comes to talking about one another.

> But now ye also put off all these: anger, wrath, malice, blasphemy, filthy communication out of your mouth (Col. 3.8).

The Bible says life and death are in the power of the tongue.

> My brethren, be not many masters, knowing that we shall receive the greater condemnation. For in many things we offend

all. If any man offend not in word, the same is a perfect man, and able also to bridle the whole body (Jas. 3.1–2).

Firstly, if your mouth is in line with God's Word, you will be able to walk in divine health. Secondly, if your mouth is in line with God's Word you will find that the body of Christ will be jointly fitted together as one. If you can control your mouth, you are a spiritual person. The Bible says out of the abundance of the heart, the mouth speaks. What you have in abundance in your heart will come out of your mouth.

One night after preaching on the love of God, I came out of the Bible study with my wife, climbed into my car and reversed into a pillar. While everybody was coming out of the Bible study, I was standing there kicking my car and the more my wife told me that everyone was watching, the harder I kicked it! Whenever you preach on the love of God, you will be given an opportunity to prove what you preach.

Behold, we put bits in the horses' mouths, that they may obey us; and we turn about their whole body. Behold also the ships, which though they be so great, and are driven of fierce winds, yet are they turned about with a very small helm, whithersoever the governor listeth. Even so the tongue is a little member, and boasteth great things. Behold, how great a matter a little fire kindleth! And the tongue is a fire, a world of iniquity: so is the tongue among our members, that it defileth the whole body, and setteth on fire the course of nature; and it is set on fire of hell (Jas. 3.3–6).

Somebody will come to you and say, 'Do you know what so-and-so said?' When you hear, you get angry and tell someone else what you think of so-and-so. Like a flame which starts small, it grows and grows until it becomes a big bonfire. If we could only start looking at people the way that God looks at us, everybody would be fine.

A source of anger is *pride*. We should realise that when we are reborn that old self dies on the cross with Jesus. A preacher once told his congregation that during one of our services, I told everybody that God had shown me that they should all sign a cheque and put it into the offering basket blank, and once I got home the Lord would reveal to me how much should be filled in on each cheque! My first reaction was to go and speak to this man but the Lord showed me to just start praying for him, he didn't know any better, and it was only my pride which wanted to get angry and have a fight.

Many people have such swollen heads that they get angry the minute anybody says anything which does not agree with what they think.

Jesus said that you would suffer persecution for His name's sake or for the Word's sake. It is fine to get drunk every night and be a woman beater *but* get saved and filled with the Holy Spirit, and start casting out devils and your whole family tells you that you have gone mad! The office staff all spoke to you while you were getting drunk at office parties, *but* once you were filled with another kind of spirit they ignored you! When they have a problem, though, in the middle of the night, or their wife leaves them, they come running to you first.

The problem with the Church has been that nobody has known the difference between the world and the Christians. We are the light, the salt of the earth, the ones with the solution, the ones to show people to Jesus, the ones who have an abundance of joy when circumstances look bad.

> A man's pride shall bring him low: but honour shall uphold the humble in spirit (Prov. 29.23).

The Bible says, 'Give and it shall be given you, good measure, pressed down and shaken together.' If you are not loved, then go and give some love. It will come back to you. Love never fails. Ken Stewart said that he had not had an argument with his wife in thirteen years of marriage, because they had the revelation that it takes two to argue, so if someone wants to fight with you, just love them.

Another source of anger is an *uncontrolled temper*. Temperance is a fruit of the Spirit and it means self control. Once you are born again you have temperance and if you will allow that temperance to run its full course through your life, you will have self control. *Anger will blind the mind* to reason and common sense. Cain slew his brother Abel through anger. *Anger demands retaliation* and wants to hurt others. Anger can make you physically ill, it can cause the organs of your body not to function.

How to rule over anger

> That ye put off concerning the former conversation the old man, which is corrupt according to the deceitful lusts; And be renewed in the spirit of your mind (Eph. 4.22–23).

You have to realise that you become a brand new creation but your physical body and mind do not get recreated. If you were bald before you were born again, you will be bald afterwards. You are going to have to put off the old man in the physical.

> And that ye put on the new man, which after God is created in righteousness and true holiness. Wherefore putting away lying, speak every man truth with his neighbour: for we are members one of another (Eph. 4.24–25).

Your word is your bond. God's Word will only be as good as your word. If you cannot believe what you say, how can you believe God's Word when you say it?

> Be ye angry, and sin not: let not the sun go down upon your wrath: Neither give place to the devil.

Faith cannot work when you are angry.

> Let him that stole steal no more: but rather let him labour, working with his hands the thing which is good, that he may

have to give to him that needeth. Let no corrupt communication proceed out of your mouth, but that which is good to the use of edifying, that it may minister grace unto the hearers. And grieve not the Holy Spirit of God, whereby ye are sealed unto the day of redemption. [When you start speaking badly of each other the Holy Ghost is grieved.]

Let all bitterness, and wrath, and anger, and clamour, and evil speaking, be put away from you, with all malice (Eph. 4.26–31).

We must speak *words of life*. If you want to rule over anger you will have to put away all evil speaking and bitterness and learn to speak words of life. There is a vocabulary of silence. If you have nothing good to say, don't say anything, just bite your lip. If someone comes to you and says, 'Do you know what so-an-so said?' say 'Praise the Lord, let's pray for them.'

We need to walk in *forgiveness*.

And be ye kind one to another, tenderhearted, forgiving one another (Eph. 4.32).

Forgiving one another. The time has come where we are being taught in the area of the spirit, the soul and the flesh, and you are going to have to realise that you are a tri-part being and that your spirit man is the real you.

Your spirit man should dominate and rule over your life. When you begin to walk in the spirit you will not fulfil the lusts of the flesh. Now I believe in deliverance but too many people think that they need deliverance when all they need to do is *get their flesh under control*.

This I say then, Walk in the Spirit (Gal. 5.16).

It means live a spirit-ruled life, be dominated by the spirit man, put your flesh under and get in line with your spirit.

> Ye shall not fulfil the lust of the flesh. For the flesh lusteth against the Spirit, and the Spirit against the flesh (Gal. 5.16–17).

You need to understand that when you are born again, your flesh is not. Your flesh has not been told that it is a new creation. Your flesh still wants to carry on as it did from the day you were born. I realised this one night. Symptoms from my body building days that had not bothered me for many years came back. I said, 'Now wait a bit, I am a new creature,' and the Spirit of God rose up inside of me and said, 'Yes, but your body does not know that, tell it!' So I said 'Body, I am a new creature in Christ Jesus, I am redeemed from the curse of the law and you had better get in line with me now in Jesus' name.' And it did. *Your body will do whatever you tell it to do*. You cannot stand up right now without telling your body to. We need to realise this.

Jerry Savelle made a commitment to God that he would spend eight hours a day in the Word for three months. He would go to bed at night and set the alarm for five a.m. The first morning the alarm went off and he just went back to sleep and woke at seven-thirty a.m. He got up and repented and asked the Lord to forgive him. The same thing happened the next morning. The following morning when the alarm went off he got up and went into the bathroom and stood on the edge of the tub and told his body that if it fell asleep it would fall and hurt itself. He did that for three or four mornings and after that he never had a problem with his body in that area again.

When you are in a meeting where faith is high and you are with a body of believers, it is great, you don't feel like sinning, you are in the spirit, you are praising God. It would be very difficult to get angry in that atmosphere, but two or three days later when the pressure is on, everybody at work is shouting, and you haven't slept well – that is when you are going to have to get your body in line with your spirit and put it under.

And these are contrary the one to the other; so that ye cannot do the things that ye would. But if ye be led of the Spirit, ye are not under the law. Now the works of the flesh are manifest, which are these; Adultery, fornication, uncleanness, lasciviousness, idolatry, witchcraft, hatred, variance, emulations, wrath, strife, seditions, heresies, envyings, murders, drunkenness, revellings, and such like: of the which I tell you before, as I have also told you in time past, that they which do such things shall not inherit the kingdom of God. But the fruit of the Spirit is love, joy, peace, longsuffering, gentleness, goodness, faith, meekness, temperance: against such there is no law (Gal. 5.17–23).

The time has come when Christians are going to live a spiritual life. There is an army of believers that are being raised up across this earth that are not being dominated by the flesh any longer. They are going forth right now and will not stand for the devil and his deceit. They are not going to allow the devil to trip them up. We must make a *quality decision* that we will refuse to speak evil or get angry and that we will walk in the Spirit. The greatest thing is to live a spirit ruled life.

6. Poverty

The truth about poverty has been fought by the devil more than any other truth and after reading this chapter you will understand why. You will understand why people get angry when we share on this subject, why religion and tradition do not like it.

Beloved, I wish above all things that thou mayest prosper and be in health (3 John 2).

Let them shout for joy, and be glad, that favour my righteous cause: yea, let them say continually, Let the Lord be magnified, which hath pleasure in the prosperity of his servant (Ps. 35.27).

Poverty is not a blessing from God and through Christ Jesus we have been redeemed from it. If someone thinks that it is a blessing when a husband who is an alcoholic runs away and leaves his wife and four children without food, then we do not serve the same God. If someone thinks that when people are starving and have nothing, they are blessed, then we do not know the same God. Of course it is better to have plenty than to have nothing. Brother Hagin said that people who have been both sick and healthy, will tell you that it is much better to be healthy. Poverty means a poorness, inadequacy, lack of needs being met.

Prosperity means the ability to meet any given need at any given time through the power of God. Prosperity is not just finances, that is only a small part. Prosperity is not a get-rich-quick scheme. The Word of God is *not* a get-rich-quick scheme – it is a way of life. You need to live the Word of God twenty-four hours a day. It is also not just money – would you exchange your eyesight for a million pounds? You can have millions of pounds but if you have cancer, you are not prosperous.

The Bible does not say that money is the root of all evil. That came from the devil in order to deceive Christians. It says *the love of money.* A person can have nothing and love money or have plenty and love it. But it is possible to be in either situation and yet not love money.

There is a story about a man called Sambo who was employed by the wealthiest man in the south of the United States of America. Sambo loved the Lord and just shone for Jesus. He tried to speak to his employer but he would not listen. One day the employer went to a meeting and a man stood up and said that he had to be obedient to the Lord. He said that God had told him that the wealthiest man in the south would die before six o'clock the next morning. The man thought that they had to be talking about him because he had more money than anybody else in the south. He called his physician and told him to spend the night with him. The physician checked him every fifteen minutes throughout the night and six o'clock came and went and he was still alive. Of course he said that they didn't know what they were talking about. Then there was a knock on the door. One of the servants asked if it would be possible for everyone to have the afternoon off because Sambo had died at five to six that morning and the funeral would be in the afternoon. The wealthiest man in the region was not wealthy through money but through Christ. Prosperity is knowing Jesus Christ and being a success with God by knowing His will and acting on it.

Poverty came with sin. Adam and Eve never lacked anything before they sinned. They had dominion, walked in fellowship with God, had never suffered sickness or pain, but after they sinned, God said that women would suffer pain in childbirth, and that men would have to till the soil. Poverty never came with God, it came with sin. The devil is the one who is causing poverty amongst the believers.

It is physically impossible to reach Africa for Jesus without billions of rands coming into the kingdom. If you have nothing, you can do nothing. This is why the devil has hindered finances in the Church. God wants you to be blessed so that you can be a blessing to others. The Bible tells us that the gospel has to be preached throughout the world before Jesus can come back. The devil is hindering us from doing the work of the ministry because the longer it takes for us to reach the world, the longer it will take for Jesus to come back. Everyone thinks that we are waiting on Jesus. No, Jesus is waiting on us to get the job done but the day of the devil deceiving the Church is over. The Christians are the ones who are going to prosper in these last days. The Christians are the ones who will get the work done.

Prosperity is not having a big fat cigar in your mouth with a bottle of champagne at your elbow and a whole hoard of money in the bank! I don't want to be selfish for Jesus – I want as much as God will give me to give others. If you have no love, you cannot give any. If you have no joy, you cannot give any. If you have no money, you cannot give any. Prosperity is standing under the shower on a Monday morning rejoicing, praising Jesus for the beautiful day and looking forward to going to work. What a privilege it is to serve Jesus Christ. He went to hell so that I don't have to. He took my sicknesses so that I don't have to be sick any more.

One of the reasons why Christians suffer poverty is *lack of knowledge*. (See also chapter 5, section 4, 'Why do Christians suffer?')

> My people are destroyed for lack of knowledge (Hos. 4.6).

We have been taught that the poorer you are, the more spiritual you are.

Many Christians do not fully understand the plan of redemption and think that they have only been redeemed from sin.

> Christ hath redeemed us from the curse of the law, being made a curse for us (Gal. 3.13).

Jesus Christ went to the cross, not only for our sins, but also so that we would not be poverty stricken or sick any more. He became our substitute and went to hell so that we would not have to go. He took our infirmities. He bore our sicknesses. By His stripes we are healed. If He took your sin then you don't have to carry your sinful nature any longer. To say that you are going to suffer poverty and sickness is the same as saying that you are going to suffer sin – *you cannot separate them.*

What people are really saying is that Jesus Christ did not do sufficient on the cross in the plan of redemption for them and so they are going to have to help Him with it. How can they think that they can suffer more to help Jesus complete the plan of redemption? They do not say that about sin. Imagine if someone said, 'I am going to sin and beat up my wife and get drunk so that I can sin a bit more because Jesus didn't do enough for me.'

The Bible says we have to suffer but we need to discern what we have to suffer. Identification and substitution are two different things (see chapter 3). You should find out what you have to identify with. Do you identify with sin? *No!* Jesus was the substitute. Do you identify with poverty, spiritual death and sickness? *No!* Jesus took it on the cross. So then what do we have to suffer? The Bible tells us we have to suffer *for the Word's sake.* When we begin to stand on the Word, persecution and affliction will arise for the Word's sake.

People come to me and say that since they started tithing, the refrigerator has broken down, someone has bumped into their car etc. etc. When your family or friends begin to ridicule you because you are speaking in tongues, laying hands on the sick and casting out devils, that is the persecution the Bible speaks of. When you stand on the Word of God, people will say that you are a fanatic. They are right – you are! People persecuted Jesus – they wanted to throw Him off a cliff, they wanted to stone Him – and the same persecution will come against you *for the Word's sake.*

> Surely he hath borne our griefs, and carried our sorrows: yet we did esteem him stricken, smitten of God, and afflicted. But he was wounded for our transgressions, he was bruised for our iniquities. [That means that if He took it, we don't have to – that is the substitution. Jesus went to hell nearly 2,000 years ago, defeated the devil, conquered sin, sickness, poverty, unrest.] The chastisement of our peace was upon him [that same word 'peace' in the Old Testament is translated 'prosperity' in Psalms] and with his Stripes we are healed (Isa.53.4–5)

Verse 10 says that it pleased the Lord to bruise Him. It pleased Him! Why? So that millions of us would not have to go through it. From that second onwards, if we stood up and said we receive Jesus Christ as Lord and Saviour, the devil and every demon on this earth could do nothing. We become born again of His Spirit. He was the firstborn from the dead. That means that there must be a second born and somewhere along the line you will find your number! That is why it pleased the Lord.

> For ye know the grace of our Lord Jesus Christ, that, though he was rich, yet for your sakes he became poor, that ye through his poverty might be rich (2 Cor. 8.9).

The word 'rich' means a full supply.

Substitution – people say that it only means spiritually. No, it doesn't. How can it mean spiritually? Jesus raised people from the dead – He was not spiritually poor. How could a man who was spiritually poor raise people from the dead?

Another reason why we suffer poverty is through tradition and religious ideas that don't line up with the Word of God. All people hear is how poverty stricken they have to be to be spiritual. How can that have anything to do with your walk with God?

How to rule over poverty

Seek first the kingdom of God. If you have your eyes on things you will not prosper. If you follow Jesus because of the fish, forget it. When I was at Bible School in Tulsa, I had a job as a cleaner in a health spa – scrubbing showers, cleaning toilets etc. But when we are in God's perfect will, we are prosperous. One day the Lord said to me, 'Son, I know that I can trust you with big things because I can trust you with small things. You are not following me because of the fish but because you love me.' I began to weep – I was a cleaning boy for a few months but I finished up running that whole place! The owner offered me several thousand dollars a month to remain there but I was itching to get the Word out – I could not wait any longer, I was ready to go. If you are in God's will, you will prosper.

Prosperity is not things. *It is knowing God.*

> And yet I say unto you, That even Solomon in all his glory was not arrayed like one of these. Wherefore, if God so clothe the grass of the field, which today is, and tomorrow is cast into the

> oven, shall He not much more clothe you, O ye of little faith? (Matt. 6.29–30).

People wonder whether it is God's will to provide for them. Would you keep your children without clothes to teach them something?

The devil has taken finances, put them in a reservoir, and kept them out of the hands of the Christians. And Christians have said, 'Oh, we don't need finances. We will reach the world with the gospel somehow.' Pornographic magazines have jet planes to get their material out and the punk rock groups have 15,000-seater stadiums for their concerts. Yet we sit back and say we will manage somehow!!

Stay humble before God. Don't reach a place where you will not listen. Don't reach a place where things begin to get in your way with God. *Please God whether anybody likes it or not.* Desire to seek Him first in every area of your life. Know that it is God's desire for you to prosper. John 10.10 tells you that the devil comes to steal, kill and destroy and that Jesus came to give us *abundant life*. It is God's desire for you to prosper so that we can establish His covenant upon this earth. It is God's will for you to prosper in joy and peace. It is God's will that you have a good marriage with obedient children.

Prosperity – joy – having no fear – living by faith – is a way of life. It is not something you pull out of a lucky dip! You have to meditate on the Word.

> This book of the law shall not depart out of thy mouth; but thou shalt meditate therein day and night, that thou mayest observe to do according to all that is written therein: for *then* thou shalt make thy way prosperous, and then thou shalt have good success (Josh. 1.8, italics mine).

> But his delight is in the law of the Lord; and in his law doth he meditate day and night. And he shall be like a tree planted by

the rivers of water, that bringeth forth his fruit in his season; his leaf also shall not wither; and whatsoever he doeth shall prosper (Ps. 1.2–3).

Just *stay* in the Word, *live* the Word, *act* the Word, *believe* the Word and God *will* prosper you.

You must apply the conditions given in the Word of God to prosper.

Give, and it shall be given unto you; good measure, pressed down, and shaken together, and running over (Luke 6.38).

Some people say that nobody loves them. It is because they do not love anybody. The Bible says give – if you want love, give love. If you want friendship, give friendship. If you want to prosper financially, give cheerfully. God does not look at what you give. He looks at your heart.

When Jesus stood by and watched the widow woman put in her offering of two little mites, He said that she had given more than anybody – she had given all she had. Some people have got millions in the bank and they give the gospel a hundred rand and think they are giving more than anybody. One night I had to hold back the tears when a black woman – part of our congregation – gave my wife an envelope toward the *Rhema News*. Inside was a beautiful letter and R2.00. Tha woman gave more than someone who earns R5,000.00 a month and gives a hundred.

In Malawi, men of God walked for days barefoot to get to the meetings where the gospel was being preached. They had half or three quarters of a Bible wrapped up in a cloth – their most valuable possession. One minister went without food for several days in order to give us an offering of R6.00.

Be a giver in every area of your life. It is more blessed to give than to receive.

For bodily exercise profiteth little: but godliness is profitable

> unto all things, having promise of the life that now is, and of that which is to come (1 Tim. 4.8).

> Will a man rob God? Yet ye have robbed me. But ye say, Wherein have we robbed thee? In tithes and offerings. Ye are cursed with a curse: for ye have robbed me, even this whole nation. Bring ye all the tithes into the storehouse, that there may be meat in mine house, and prove me now herewith, saith the Lord of hosts, if I will not open you the windows of heaven, and pour you out a blessing, that there shall not be room enough to receive it. And I will rebuke the devourer for your sakes, and he shall not destroy the fruits of your ground; neither shall your vine cast her fruit before the time in the field, saith the Lord of hosts (Mal. 3.8–11).

The issue is not what you have. Many people with swimming pools and tennis courts love God more than people who live in tin shacks. The issue is not what you have, but what you have inside your heart. Don't keep your eyes on things. God will bless you if you are a giver.

You must be in the will of God in your own personal life to prosper. Some of you are confessing, complaining, jumping up and down, but until you are in the will of God in your own personal life, you will not prosper.

> If ye abide in me and my words abide in you, ye shall ask what ye will, and it shall be done unto you. Here in is my Father glorified, that ye bear much fruit; so shall ye be my disciples (John 15.7–8).

Prophecy that came forth after this teaching

For you see it has always been the way of the world, the way of the world, the way of the world. But you see ways are changing in these last days. I sent My Son and He has done the work, He has done the full work and it was done in the earth, and it was done legally in the earth. So it is time now for you to realise that you have to rise up and take, rise up and take. Why did I tell you to occupy till I come, why did I tell you to occupy? I told you to be the shepherd of this earth, all of you. I told you to take dominion over all the things that are in this earth. You know I set it in motion from the very start. Why do you think I produced and formed you from dirt? I placed your human spirit which is able to multiply whatever it conceives and I wrapped it in a foil and a fold of the most productive thing on your planet, dirt. Anything conceived inside your heart will spring forth because it has to. When you place that seed in the dirt it grows. That is why I made you the way I made you. But you are just now beginning to get a hold of it, but you are going to have to get bold in it. There are many things out there I have for you. I invented all those plans for you.

I gave you all the material on the face of this earth, to build these buildings to house my people. I have given you the knowledge in the earth, but you see it has been perverted by Satan's crowd, but it is time you took it back. It is time you realise there is no lack. I didn't bring lack. I brought a full supply and I have given it to you, but you must do the same thing that all men have had to do, you must gain that information. You must use much meditation and then you must use application. The information is in my Word, the meditation, well, that has to be done by you, but you are not doing that, you are not doing that. And then after it is conceived in your heart you have to do it, you have to apply it, that is why you sit in this place today. My servant and his wife did things this way, they gained the information, they did the meditation and you are sitting in the application. You are starting – you haven't even taken dominion over your nation yet. The rest of the Continent is out there, and I am placing upon you this day, and it is being placed upon you in this way – you will rise up and go forth from this place and you will cover this Continent all over its entire face. It is being placed upon you now, as a truth and vow it will come out of here and it will be through those that will hear and hear and hear and go forth and do it and do it and do it. But you will have to do it, you will have to take it and you will have to do it, you will have to get my Word and you will have to chew it. But I am placing that upon this place and you will see it come to pass. It will be something that is going to last, it will be for ever more. There is an effectual door open here that people will look toward and see from all over the face of the entire earth. Men are beginning to notice, they are beginning to take notice. No, not of him, of you. It is my people. So rise up behind this !eader that I have given you. Oh, I have given you one that will do it, rise up behind him, hear what he says, do what he does. He is just a copy cat. He is only doing what Paul said. You see, he is trying to act like Paul, who tried to act like Jesus, who acts like Me. So you act like him and you take this place from end to end, absolutely take it and possess it, possess it for Me!

7. Disappointment

The word 'disappointment' means to fail to satisfy an expectation. Disappointment will always be on this earth. It is not what happens. It is how we react to what happens. Disappointment can, if allowed to affect you, destroy your faith. I have seen people get so turned on to the Word of God and then get into a business deal, or believe for something and when things don't come right in the first week, they get disappointed and their faith disappears. I have seen people float on a cloud for a couple of weeks and suddenly, when things don't work out exactly as they want them, they get disappointed.

It can also cause people to backslide. I have seen more people backslide through disappointment than anything else. Disappointment in preachers. People say, 'Well, if that man is supposed to be a preacher then I think this whole thing is rubbish,' and I have seen people so disappointed in other Christians that they turn their back on the Lord Jesus Christ. Even if every preacher went out and got drunk, the Word of God does not change and nor should you. Our faith is in the rock, and the rock does not change.

I have seen people, through sin, become disappointed with everything in life. Judas' evil heart for gain brought forth his death. I have so many people coming to me and saying, 'I just wish that I had never committed adultery. It broke up my marriage and ruined my family.' Sin will destroy you. It may be fun for a season but after that it will destroy you.

Unfounded or imagined disappointment is common, especially in the Body of Christ. The disciples thought that Jesus was dead and they were disappointed.

> But we trusted that it had been he which should have redeemed Israel: and beside all this, today is the third day since these things were done (Luke 24.21).

The first time I was given the opportunity to go to the United States as a Christian, I was to be taken around to give my testimony on some of the television networks and then give a body building display. One of the reasons I wanted to go was because I knew that God had called me to go to Tulsa to Bible School so I decided that while I was there God would arrange for me to attend Bible School a couple of weeks later, and my wife – with a miracle – would join me. At the time she did not want to know about me going into the ministry. Anyway I went all the way to America, went to the Bible School and found that there was no one to see me! If you have travelled thousands of miles to meet someone who was not there, you will understand how I felt. I had expected to see Kenneth Hagin, Jr. who was the Head of the School, and he wasn't there! *I was disappointed.* But later the Lord sent him to stay in our home in Johannesburg and he gave my wife a free bursary to the school.

Mary and Martha thought that Lazarus was physically dead until the final resurrection. They were disappointed when the Master never came while he was alive. They did not know that He was going to raise Lazarus from the dead.

> Then Martha, as soon as she heard that Jesus was coming, went and met him: but Mary sat still in the house. Then said Martha unto Jesus, Lord, if thou hadst been here, my brother had not died. But I know, that even now, whatsoever thou wilt ask of God, God will give it thee (John 11.20–22).

They knew God was able to do anything. The question is not whether God is able – the question is always whether God is willing. *He is just as willing as He is able.* Praise God!

> Jesus saith unto her, Thy brother shall rise again. Martha saith unto him, I know that he shall rise again in the resurrection at the last day (John 11.23–24).

Most Christians will agree with you about the future. 'Oh, Hallelujah, one day in the sweet by-and-by – some day Jesus will do it' – but God works in the *now*.

Then there are those who are always talking about what God did years ago.

'Jesus said unto her, I am…' Not I have been, or I will be, but I AM. I AM the One who will raise Lazarus from the dead. I AM the I AM that divided the Red Sea. I AM the I AM that changed the water into wine. I AM the I AM that spoke to the wind and the wind ceased.

> I am the resurrection, and the life: he that believeth in me, though he were dead, yet shall he live. And whosoever liveth and believeth in me shall never die. Believest thou this? (John 11.25–26).

He asked her a straightforward question. Do you believe that I am the resurrection and the life? Do you believe that if you believe in Me you will never die? She tried to spiritualise it. She would not answer the question.

She saith unto him, Yea, Lord: I believe that thou art the Christ, the Son of God, which should come into the world. [That had nothing to do with the question.]

Jesus said, Take ye away the stone. Martha, the sister of him that was dead, saith unto him, Lord, by this time he stinketh: for he hath been dead four days (John 11.27, 39). [Is it easier to raise someone after they have been dead for one, two or three days?!]

How to rule over disappointment

Firstly, do not put your trust in man but in Christ Jesus. Don't ever put your trust in any human being – put it in God. Once your trust is in the Lord Jesus Christ then you are on the right track. You can put your trust in us to lead spiritually but I am talking about people wanting only one person to pray for them. Jesus is the Healer.

> The Lord is my rock, and my fortress, and my deliverer; my God, my strength, in whom I will trust; my buckler, and the horn of my salvation, and my high tower (Ps. 18.2).

> It is better to trust in the Lord than to put confidence in man. It is better to trust in the Lord than to put confidence in princes (Ps. 118.8–9).

People say they have their confidence in the Lord and then they lose their job and have a nervous breakdown – children of the living God and yet they are reduced to begging bread. If God has to bring a raven to meet your need, He will. When you trust God, sink or swim, you will swim every time because He will throw out that life jacket to you.

Ninety per cent of people blame others for their own backsliding. When you stand before the Lord on the day of judgement, He will ask what you have done, not what your best friend did! You can't tell Him that the guy who lived next door and called himself a Christian, but was crooked, caused you to backslide!

Secondly, take your disappointments to Christ and leave them there.

> Humble yourselves therefore under the mighty hand of God, that he may exalt you in due time: Casting all your care upon him; for he careth for you (1 Pet. 5.6–7).

God knows your future better than you know your past and God knows what is in your heart – when you leave your care at the Lord's feet, you allow Him to handle it. There are some disappointments that have to be left with the Lord. There is no way in the natural that you can overcome them. That is why you must look to Jesus for your strength, joy, peace and patience to overcome disappointments. Draw your strength from Jesus.

> But we had the sentence of death in ourselves, that we should not trust in ourselves, but in God which raiseth the dead (2 Cor. 1.9).

I don't trust myself (I do not mean my spirit man). I don't trust my flesh – I will not go out at midnight to counsel a girl on my own, it would be foolish. A preacher friend of mine fell into that trap. Always take someone with you.

Do not be swayed by adverse circumstances which try to defeat you – that is where major disappointment comes from. In Acts 16, Paul and Silas were beaten and thrown into prison for preaching the Gospel but they just began praising God.

Instead of thinking about your problem, take your mind and eyes off it, and put them on Jesus. Let Jesus solve the problem. You could not solve it on your own anyway so what is the point of trying to work it out? Just go to Jesus and let Him find the solution.

John Bunyan wrote *The Pilgrim's Progress* in jail. He could have sat there crying but instead he wrote one of the greatest spiritual books ever written. No matter what happens in life we are more than conquerors through Christ Jesus. Whatever disappointments come my way, I will put my trust in the Word of God and I will overcome every one of them through Jesus Christ, *and so will you.*

Psalm 91 is my favourite Psalm. I confess it over my family and my life continually. Begin to speak the Word over your circumstances. Begin to come against them. *Don't be a half-hearted Christian. Stand up and be counted.*

> He that dwelleth in the secret place of the most High shall abide under the shadow of the Almighty. I will say of the Lord, he is my refuge and my fortress: my God; in him will I trust [I will say of the Lord – I will *confess* – that he is my fortress, my refuge, in him will I trust.] Surely he shall deliver thee from the snare of the fowler, and from the noisome pestilence. He shall cover thee with his feathers, and under his wings shalt thou trust: his truth shall be thy shield and buckler. Thou shalt not be afraid... (Ps. 91.1–5).

Thou shalt not be afraid. When I become aware that a spirit of fear is trying to come on me, I immediately begin to confess, 'I have not got a spirit of fear, but a spirit of power and love and a sound mind.' I chase the devil down the street right out of the area! The devil attacks preachers the same as anybody else – we get the same symptoms.

We need to have faith for every day – you need to meditate and get into the Word of God *daily*.

> Thou shalt not be afraid for the terror by night; nor for the arrow that flieth by day (Ps. 91.5).

He is saying that we should not pay any attention to rumours of wars or even the wars themselves. If we abide under the shadow of the Almighty, they will fly right past us.

> Nor for the pestilence that walketh in darkness [that is Satan and his demons] nor for the destruction that wasteth at noonday. A thousand shall fall at thy side, and ten thousand at thy right hand; but it shall not come nigh thee. Only with thine eyes shalt thou behold and see the reward of the wicked. Because thou hast made the Lord, which is my refuge, even the most high, thy habitation. There shall no evil befall thee, neither shall any plague come nigh thy dwelling.
>
> For he shall give his angels charge over thee, to keep thee in all thy ways. They shall bear thee up in their hands, lest thou dash thy foot against a stone. Thou shalt tread upon the lion and adder: the young lion and the dragon shalt thou trample under feet. [When you speak to the devil, look down not up, he is under your feet!] Because he hath set his love upon me, therefore will I deliver him (Ps. 91.6–14).

There are people who need a miracle. God says He will deliver you because you have set your love upon Him. He will deliver you because you have stood on His Word and the circumstances will change. *God will deliver you.*

4
Identification and substitution

1. Identification

I am sure that every born-again believer desires to identify with the Head of the Church, the Lord Jesus Christ. Yes, most Christians want to identify with Jesus, but, unfortunately, a lot of people seem to identify with the wrong things.

Now, the world desires to identify with Satan. I am sure many of you can remember how you identified with the devil, albeit not always knowingly, before you were born again. I know that I did during the early part of my life, until the age of twenty. I acted like him, I was obedient to him, I did everything that he put into my head to do; I did not always realise where it came from, but whether you realise it or not: you either identify with God through Jesus Christ, or with Satan. You also need to realise that that is the reason why Jesus had to come to earth. Satan was our stepfather, but when we were born again, we took on a new nature. Jesus Christ came into our lives. He became the Lord of our lives and God became our Father.

> And you hath he quickened, who were dead in trespasses and sins; Wherein in time past ye walked according to the course of this world, according to the prince of the power of the air, the spirit that now worketh in the children of disobedience: Among whom also we had our conversation in times past in the lusts of

our flesh, fulfilling the desires of the flesh and of the mind; and were by nature the children of wrath, even as others (Eph. 2.1–3).

Does that sound like you before you were born again?

Some of us, when we saw Marlon Brando on that big motor-bike in the film *The Wild Ones*, and when we saw other films like *Easy Rider* and *Hell's Angels*, started to identify with all that stuff. Where do you think they got all that from, in any case? Hell's Angels, indeed! When you have the divine nature of God, you start to identify with the God whom you serve; but there are people going around murdering, killing and doing the most satanic things because they identify with the god whom they serve, namely Satan.

But God, who is rich in mercy, for his great love wherewith he loved us, Even when we were dead in sins, hath quickened us together with Christ, (by grace ye are saved;) And hath raised us up together, and made us sit together in heavenly places in Christ Jesus (Eph. 2.4–6).

The word 'Christian' means one who is Christ-like; it means 'little anointed ones'. When we are born again and filled with the Spirit of God, and as we begin to walk according to the Word, we begin to identify with God and Jesus Christ, and we begin to walk as 'little anointed ones': that is, Christ-like. Tragically, there are people in the body of Christ today who are still identifying with the wrong things. Christians are not running around identifying with the devil and the lusts of the flesh, but some are identifying with the wrong things. I want to show you from the Word of God what we are to identify with.

Persecution

Remember the word that I said unto you, The servant is not

> greater than his lord. If they have persecuted me, they will also persecute you (John 15.20).

The servant is not greater than his lord; so one thing we can always expect is to suffer persecution on the earth, until Jesus returns. I heard someone say that we who are in the 'Faith' churches teach that as soon as you receive Jesus, all your troubles are over with and all you do is walk on a cloud of candy-floss. That is not what we teach at all. The Bible says that whosoever is born of God overcometh this world, so when persecution and affliction arrive, we teach you how to overcome it. I want to tell you now that persecution and affliction will always come: if Jesus suffered persecution, we are going to suffer it as well.

> And have no root in themselves and so endure but for a time: afterward, when affliction or persecution ariseth for the word's sake, immediately they are offended (Mark 4.17).

If you are not being persecuted, you are not walking in the Word. The more Word you are walking in, the more the devil will come against you, but, praise God, you can do exactly what Jesus did: you can say, 'It is written.' You can defeat the devil on this earth; you do not have to wait until you get to heaven, as some people expect to do: 'Boy, am I going to give it to the devil when I get to heaven!' Forget it; he is not going to be in heaven, in any case!

The Bible says that we have been delivered from the dominion of darkness and translated into the kingdom of His dear Son. I do not serve the devil any more. He is not my god and he has nothing to do with me. He cannot come into my house or on to my property, he cannot touch my finances or the anointing that God has laid upon my life. I am not a citizen of this earth any more; I have to live in it, but I am not of it: I am an ambassador for Jesus, for heaven, and ambassadors do not normally live in their own countries, they live in a foreign country. I live in a country (earth) which is not my home any more – it is an enemy-occupied country and I am my Lord's special agent; every time I listen to a church service, I am listening to news from my country (heaven), giving me instructions how to operate in this enemy country. The devil will try and keep me from going to church, by laying traps in my way, by persecution and affliction: he will try, but if you are wearing your armour, fitted as prescribed in Ephesians 6.14–20, the devil will be like a big bull-dog without teeth: all bark and no bite. He had his teeth removed 2,000 years ago when Jesus defeated him. You can use the name of Jesus to defeat the devil in every situation – that is the one thing the devil cannot stand up to: the name of Jesus.

We identify with persecution and affliction for the Word's sake. I know of people in my parish who have been persecuted by their wives, their husbands or other members of their family. Sometimes I think that must be one of the hardest things: when someone you love very much does not understand what you are doing or why you are doing it though to you it is the most important thing in your life. It can become much harder to bear than any physical suffering.

Jesus became our substitute on the cross and, because He did, we do not have to suffer sickness, disease and sin any more. (See also, chapter 1, section 8, on Paul's thorn in the flesh.) It is a tragedy that most Christians think that Jesus did not do enough for them on the cross. They think that if they suffer sickness, they can complete what Jesus did on the cross for them. That is egoistic and it comes from the pits of hell; Satan is trying to convince people that they need to be sick – they accept salvation from the cross of Jesus, but not healing for the body. If you tried for a billion years to do one iota of what Jesus did on the cross, you could not do it. God gave His only begotten Son, who knew no sin, for us, so that we can be set free.

I do not care what comes against you. When you take the Word of God and you begin to use it, no matter what your circumstances are or how bleak or black the situation looks, if you stand on the Word of God, the Lord will deliver you out of all. Do not compromise: put on the armour of God so that you may be able to stand.

2. Substitution

We have had a look at what we need to identify with; now let us look at Jesus, our substitution. If I tell you that I have gone down the street and paid every account that you had outstanding and you reply: 'Thank you very much, praise God!' but the next morning you go the same stores, exactly the same places, and tell them that you want to pay your account, people will really think that you are very dumb. Well, the Lord spoke to me and told me that that is exactly what Christians are doing. The shopkeeper is the devil and he just keeps on making them pay over and over for the same thing that Jesus already paid for 2,000 years ago. What we should be doing is going to that store and saying, 'Mr Outfitter, I want you to know that this account has been paid and I owe you nothing and you have nothing to do with me any more and you have got no hold on me, so leave me alone!' Some of us keep right on paying the same account over and over. You need to receive the fullness of His work on the cross at Calvary and apply it to your life.

> For he hath made him to be sin for us, who knew no sin; that we might be made the righteousness of God in him (2 Cor. 5.21).

He was our substitution – He was made sin – He was our sin-substitution, that we might be made the righteousness of God. A lot of Christians will not identify with the righteousness of God, they will rather identify with sin. They say: 'I am just a sinner, I am just no good, a worm in the dust, I will never amount to anything.' Some people, in false humility, will fight with you if you tell them you are the righteousness of God, because they are still identifying with the wrong things. I will not identify with sin, because Jesus was made sin for me. He was our substitute. If an instrument was made to be a piano, it cannot be an organ. It was made to be a piano, it will always be a piano and it will never be anything else, because it was made to be a piano. Well, Jesus took our sins away and made us the righteousness of God, and that is the way we are going to stay.

I want to ask you something else now. Would you ever say that Jesus did not do enough on the cross to redeem us from our sins? Would you ever say that we have to sin a little bit more to complete what He did on the cross? Yet, that is what people are saying about sickness and disease. If you say that you are taking your sickness on yourself to complete what Jesus did on the cross, you may just as well say that you are sinning a little bit more and you are taking sin upon you, so that you can complete what Jesus did on the cross concerning sin. Nowhere in the Bible can you separate healing and salvation from the plan of redemption.

Let us look at Isaiah chapter fifty-three in the Amplified Bible:

> Surely He has borne our griefs – sickness, weakness and distress – and carried our sorrows and pain of punishment...(verse 4).

God's invitation is: 'Let the weak say, I am strong' (Joel 3.10); Paul said: 'When I am weak, then am I strong' (2 Cor. 12.10). Substitution means that He gave up heaven and went to hell so that we do not have to go to hell but may go to heaven. It means Jesus carried our sorrows and pain of punishment.

> Yet we ignorantly considered Him stricken, smitten and afflicted by God as if with leprosy. But He was wounded for our transgressions, He was bruised for our iniquities (verses 4–5).

You do not have guilt any more, because He took our guilt – He was our substitute for us; is it not wonderful? There is therefore no condemnation in Christ Jesus.

> The chastisement needful to obtain peace and well-being for us was upon Him, and with the stripes that wounded Him we are healed and made whole...Yet it was the will of the Lord to bruise Him (verses 5, 10).

We should be walking in peace and well-being, because He went to the cross for that purpose. Now, God is not perverted; it was not God's will to see His only begotten Son, who is now the firstborn from the dead, put on a cross with thorns on His head and have Him crucified, because God felt like it. No, look what it says:

> Yet it was the will of the Lord to bruise Him; He has put Him to grief and made Him sick.

Why was it the will of the Lord? So that we do not have to be sick any more. I want you to realise that since Jesus rose from the dead the devil has no right to put any sickness on us, because Jesus became our substitute on the cross and carried it for us. We have been signing for accounts and packages that were paid 2,000 years ago. The Bible says 'My people are destroyed for lack of knowledge' (Hos. 4.6). Some of us lack the knowledge of what Jesus did on the cross for us. The minute you get that knowledge to be alive in your spirit the devil will never be able to deceive you as far as sickness is concerned. During the first five years of my Christian life, I thought that I needed to suffer everything because God was moulding me. All that I was moulded into was a backslider. All I said was: 'Well, God, if you want it this way, that's fine, whatever will be will be.' I lost all my health studios, never had a penny and I was not in the will of God, because I had backslidden and I started saying that the gospel does not work; but when I found out what Jesus did for me and let it get down into my spirit, that changed everything.

Isaiah goes on:

> When you and He make Him an offering for sin and He has risen from the dead, in time to come, He shall see His spiritual offspring, He shall prolong His days, and the will and pleasure of the Lord shall prosper in His hand (verse 10).

I am not going to identify with sickness. Are you?

> Bless the Lord, O my soul: and all that is within me, bless his holy name.
>
> Bless the Lord, O my soul, and forget not all his benefits (Ps. 103.1–2).

What are His benefits? Let us look at verse three:

> Who forgiveth all thine iniquities...

That is substitution for sin – He became sin that we might not know any of it – and then what else?

> Who healeth all thy diseases, Who redeemeth thy life from destruction; who crowneth thee with lovingkindness and tender mercies; Who satisfieth thy mouth with good things; so that thy youth is renewed like the eagle's (verses 3–5).

You cannot separate sickness and sin from what Jesus did on the cross for us. He substituted for us to give us health and spiritual life. If He took our sin, He also took our sicknesses.

> That it might be fulfilled which was spoken by Esaias the prophet, saying, Himself took our infirmities, and bare our sicknesses (Matt. 8.17).

> Who his own self bare our sins in his own body on the tree, that we, being dead to sins, should live unto righteousness: by whose stripes ye were healed (1 Pet. 2.24).

He took my sin so that I could live unto righteousness. He became sin so that we might be made the righteousness of God, but He does not stop there – it is not just for spiritual death, that we can be made spiritually alive, it is also to eliminate sickness, so that we can walk in divine health.

We have seen that He took upon Himself sin that we might be made the righteousness of God, that we might have eternal life; that we can be born again; that we can have spiritual life and He took sickness, so that we might walk in divine health. Now let us look at financial prosperity. (See also chapter 3, section 6, 'Poverty'.) The devil has sold us the lie about staying poor for so many years that many people find it difficult to accept that God wants us to prosper financially.

> For you are coming progressively to be acquainted with and to recognise more strongly and clearly the grace of our Lord Jesus Christ – His kindness, His gracious generosity, His undeserved favour and spiritual blessing; in that though He was so very rich, yet for your sakes He became so very poor, in order that by His poverty you might become enriched – abundantly supplied (2 Cor. 8.9, Amplified Bible).

The word 'rich' means abundantly supplied or a full supply. Some people try to tell us that the above Scripture only refers to being spiritually rich; yet it refers to Jesus being or becoming very poor. How could a very poor spiritual man raise someone from the dead?

Secondly, if you are still convinced that it is only spiritual richness, the Bible tells us that we have been blessed with all spiritual blessings and that Jesus prayed: 'Let your will be done on earth as it is in heaven.' Do you believe that heaven has got everything, that it is abundantly supplied, or do you think that it is a poor place, where people go around begging, where there is never enough of anything? If Jesus prayed 'Let it be done on earth as in heaven,' how do you think He wants it to be down here? The same as in heaven, surely: abundantly supplied.

The Word of God says that He is 'able to do exceeding abundantly above all that we ask or think, according to the power that worketh in us' (Eph. 3.20). That is one of the most forceful passages in the Word of God.

Christians have at last begun to see that God sent His Son, Jesus, to the cross so that He might become poor so that we might be made rich and have a full supply. He wants us to prosper: to prosper means to be able to meet every given situation without going under: that is what God wants the Body of Christ to do.

When we give to the gospel, God can in return bless us; the more He blesses us, the more we can put into the gospel and the more we put into the gospel, the more God can continue to bless us and the more He continues to bless us, the more we can put into the gospel. That is why God wants us to prosper, not to hoard and keep things to ourselves, but to get the gospel out to others. I want to assure you that while we do that we will stay in the will of God, and the devil's days will be numbered.

5
God's will concerning suffering

We have already seen that God does not desire that Christians should suffer sickness, poverty and distress. But this is such an important subject and gives Christians so many problems, that I want to look at it again, in more detail.

1. The teaching of God's Word

One of the reasons why there is so much confusion with regard to the subject of suffering is that in the past most people have looked to other sources for the answers. But our Answer Book is the Word of God. We must look at the Word and nothing else, and then we must interpret our suffering according to the Word of God instead of making the mistake of interpreting the Word of God according to our suffering.

Tradition and religion have swept across the Christian world like a flood but we have not been told what the Word says. The Word of God has a sure answer. In fact, Peter said that even though he saw Jesus Christ with Moses and Elijah on the Mount of Transfiguration – even so, he had a more sure way (2 Pet. 1.19). That way is the Word of God.

We have the same sure way. It should not matter what experience you have had, or what experience I have had, unless it is according to the Word of God.

Let us switch off our religious minds and learn from the

Spirit of God. The Holy Spirit has come to guide us into all truth. As you open your spirit to the Spirit of God you will realise that you do not need to stay in bondage. Most people base their relationship with God on circumstances and tradition instead of on the Word of God. One of the biggest problems we have had in the Church is people saying, 'Mrs Jones down the road suffered and she loved God,' or 'Auntie Mary went through so much and she loved Jesus.' Let us rather look at the Word of God.

> Wherefore let them that suffer according to the will of God commit the keeping of their souls to him in well doing, as unto a faithful Creator (1 Pet. 4.19).

If there is a suffering according to the will of God, then there must also be a suffering that is not according to the will of God. This is an area where we need to gain more understanding. The following is an excerpt from a certain publication:

> While in a certain place, she prayed for the grace to share in Christ's suffering. Her wish was granted. She became the prey to severe pain in her head, which was extended to her right eye. They sent her to a doctor who plucked out her eye without any anaesthetic. With all simplicity and meekness, and with the blood still flowing from her eye, she thanked the doctor and offered him a fee.
>
> She spent the night in great anguish and the following day they took her for treatment to stop the eye from haemorrhaging.
>
> She was moved to a place where she became blind, crippled and bedridden. She felt pain in her whole body which was plagued by wounds. Her knees became locked and immovable. The flesh in her open side decayed and her joints became loose. Her bones tore apart and became riddled like a porous sponge. Her skin split in a manner that you could count her vertebrae, one by one, and see the very movement of her lungs, as well as the shaking of her nerves.

> She prayed nightly in honour of the five wounds of our Lord and reminded Him of the sixth wound on his shoulder on which He carried the heavy cross of our sins. She herself carried such a wound which bled for five years. She continually smiled happily because of the partaking of the sufferings of Christ.

This kind of suffering is not according to the will of God.

Many people in the Body of Christ believe that it makes them more spiritual and more holy to suffer physically. They believe the more pain they endure, the more they are serving Jesus. This belief has prevented countless numbers of unsaved people from coming to the Lord. This is not the abundant life Jesus came to give us.

The fact is – no suffering comes from God!

Paul said that Christ has redeemed us from the curse of the law (Gal. 3.13). The curse of the law is poverty, sickness and spiritual death. Therefore, Christ has redeemed us from poverty, sickness and spiritual death. He became sin for us that we might be made the righteousness of God in Him (2 Cor. 5.21). He carried our pains and our grief that we might walk in abundant life. How dare anyone say today that Jesus Christ did not suffer enough for us; that we need to suffer more?

God sent Jesus to suffer for you and for me and Jesus said, 'It is finished.' It was over, completed on the cross.

> Who will have all men to be saved, and to come unto the knowledge of the truth (1 Tim. 2.4).

Many people are saved, but have not come to the knowledge of the truth:

> Then said Jesus to those Jews which believed on him, If you continue in my Word, then ye are my disciples indeed; And ye shall know the truth and the truth shall make you free (John 8.31–32).

It is the truth of God's Word that makes us free.

2. Suffering for the name of Jesus

There are three basic facts we need to understand in the Bible.

(a) The character and nature of God

> Jesus saith unto them, My meat is to do the will of him that sent me, and to finish his work (John 4.34).

> Jesus cried and said, He that believeth on me, believeth not on me, but on him that sent me. And he that seeth me seeth him that sent me (John 12.44–45).

> Jesus saith unto him, I am the way, the truth, and the life: no man cometh unto the Father, but by me. If ye had known me, ye should have known my Father also: and from henceforth ye know him, and have seen him. Philip saith unto him, Lord; shew us the Father, and it sufficeth us. Jesus saith unto him, Have I been so long time with you, and yet hast thou not known me, Philip? He that hath seen me hath seen the Father; and how sayest thou then, Shew us the Father? (John 14.6–9).

When Jesus lived on earth, the Pharisees and Sadducees could not understand how He could call God 'Father'. They could not understand when He said 'God is good.' Many people today have the same problem. They serve God from fear and not in love. I serve God because I love Him, because He set me free and without Him I am nothing. He gave me Eternal Life with the Father, and I love Him because of that.

(b) We must know who our enemy is

Satan is the enemy. He is the thief. He is the one who comes to kill, steal and destroy (John 10.10). He is the evil one.

(c) We need to know who we are in Christ

The Word of God grants us certain privileges as Christians, born again by the Spirit of God. We are redeemed from the curse of the law (Gal. 3.13) and heir to all the promises of God. We are the righteousness of God in Christ (2 Cor. 5.21).

Next we must realise that there are only two reasons why we are to suffer according to the Word of God.

(i) We will suffer for the name of Jesus.

> If ye be reproached for the name of Christ, happy are ye; for the Spirit of glory and of God resteth upon you (1 Pet. 4.14).

If we are reproached, if we suffer persecution for the name of Jesus, the Spirit of God rests on us. We will suffer persecution for the name of Christ as long as we live. In your job or your home, for instance, you will be persecuted for the name of Christ.

After I made a commitment to Jesus Christ, while I was still in the health studio business, people would come in and call me 'Joshua' or 'Moses', and attempt to ridicule me for the name of Jesus. But happy are we when we suffer persecution for the name of Jesus Christ. When people criticise and talk about us, then we can be happy because we know that the anointing of God rests upon us.

(ii) We will suffer persecution and affliction for the Word's sake: 'when affliction or persecution ariseth for the Word's sake...' (Mark 4.17).

When you begin to give the Word of God its rightful place in your life, and to walk in the Word, and speak the Word, and live the Word, persecution and affliction will arise.

When Jesus called the disciples and they followed Him, they suffered persecution. Some were disowned by their families, who actually had a burial for them. Thay were considered to be dead.

And many times our families react in a similar way.

Many times when people begin to live for God, the devil will try to attack them in every area he can. People have said, 'I finally started living for God, and ever since, more things have gone wrong than ever before.' When this situation arises, we can count it all joy. We can boldly confess all that God has done for us and watch the adverse circumstances change.

Also, many have said, 'Yes, but I believe it is God's will for me to suffer, so if a sickness comes along, I will just have to suffer.' Well, if it is God's will for them to be ill, they should not go to a doctor, because then they might get better and it would not be God's will!

3. Sickness, oppression, depression and poverty

Hebrews 1.3 tells us that Jesus is the express image of God on the earth. And in John 4.34 Jesus said, 'My meat is to do the will of him that sent me...'

Jesus did the will of God on earth.

> Jesus cried and said, He that believeth on me believeth not on me, but on him that sent me. And he that seeth me seeth him that sent me (John 12.44–45).

> Jesus saith unto him, I am the Way, the Truth, and the Life: no man cometh unto the Father, but by me. If ye had known me, ye should have known my Father also: and from henceforth ye know him, and have seen him. Philip saith unto him, Lord, shew us the Father, and it sufficeth us. Jesus saith unto him, Have I been so long time with you, and yet hast thou not known me, Philip? He that hath seen me hath seen the Father; and how sayest thou then, Shew us the Father? (John 14.6–9).

In other words, Jesus was saying to Philip, 'What you have seen me do is what the Father does, what He does,

I do. The way He acts, I act. He acts the same way I act. He and I are One.'

> How God anointed Jesus of Nazareth with the Holy Ghost and with power: who went about doing good, and healing all that were oppressed of the devil; for God was with him (Acts 10.38).

Jesus healed everyone who came to Him. He never refused anyone healing. He never turned to anyone and said, 'Well, I think that lump on your neck should stay,' or 'I believe it will do you some good to be in pain,' or 'That leprosy, when your toes and fingers fall off, will be a great testimony to God – I think you should stay that way.' *No, no, no, He never said that.* Jesus said:

> The Spirit of the Lord is upon me, because he hath anointed me to preach the gospel to the poor; he hath sent me to heal the brokenhearted, to preach deliverance to the captives, and recovering of sight to the blind, to set at liberty them that are bruised, to preach the acceptable year of the Lord (Luke 4.18–19).

If the men in the synagogue that day had received those words, they would have been set free, but instead, they wanted to kill Jesus. Affliction and persecution arise for the Word's sake.

There were times, when the healing power of God was manifested in Paul's ministry, that the people would attempt to stone him and chase him out of town. When Peter ministered to the lame man and he was healed, the religious people had him imprisoned.

A spirit of religion has kept the Body of Christ in bondage and locked us into tradition where we have been taught unbelief and not the Word of God.

Jesus said,

> The thief cometh not but for to steal, and to kill, and to destroy: I am come that they might have life, and that they might have it more abundantly (John 10.10).

Jesus was not confused about what He was saying. He knew the will of the Father because He and the Father were one. Jesus came to set us free and give us abundant life.

> And it came to pass, when he was in a certain city, behold a man full of leprosy: who seeing Jesus fell on his face, and besought him, saying, Lord, *if thou wilt*, thou canst make me clean. And he put forth his hand, and touched him, saying, *I will*: be thou clean. And immediately the leprosy departed from him (Luke 5.12–13, italics mine).

Many people today know God is able but they do not know if He is willing.

God is just as willing as He is able. Jesus said in verse 13 'I will.' If God healed one person, it is His will to heal all because God is no respecter of persons (Acts 10.34 and Rom. 2.11).

> ...himself took our infirmities and bare our sicknesses (Matt. 8.17).

Either He bore our sicknesses or He didn't. Either He took our infirmities or He didn't. The Word says He took our infirmities and bore our sicknesses, so that means we should not have to suffer sickness.

Jesus loves us. He went to the cross for us.

> Surely he hath borne our griefs, and carried our sorrows: yet we did esteem him stricken, smitten of God, and afflicted. But he was wounded for our transgressions, he was bruised for our iniquities: the chastisement of our peace was upon him; and with his stripes we are healed (Isa. 53.4–5).

He bore our griefs. He carried our sorrows. He was wounded for our transgressions. By His stripes we are healed. Jesus Christ finished it once and for all. What He did on the cross was a total work. It was completed.

He has redeemed us from the curse of the law. We have been blessed with all spiritual blessings. We are to prosper and be in health even as our soul prospers. We are more than conquerors in Christ Jesus and we are victorious in every situation.

4. Why do Christians suffer?

(a) Lack of knowledge

The main reason why Christians suffer things not intended for them to suffer is lack of knowledge.

Jesus Christ went to the cross to deliver us from sickness, poverty and spiritual death. But tradition and religion have hoodwinked us into believing anything except the Word of God.

> My people are destroyed for lack of knowledge (Hos. 4.6).

'My people' – not the world, but God's people.

> Therefore my people are gone into captivity, because they have no knowledge (Isa. 5.13).

Notice again, it is 'my people' – God's people.

> ...but through knowledge shall the just be delivered (Prov. 11.9).

A story I once heard illustrates this very well. A man bought a ticket for a boat voyage from America to England. It was quite a long journey, and the man realised after he had purchased his ticket that he didn't have enough money left for his meals during the trip. So he took what money he had and bought bread and cheese to eat while on board ship. When the cruise was under way, the man would pass by the dining room every mealtime and he would look through the window at the people eating and enjoying their meals. He would gaze inside and say to himself, 'If I just had enough money to pay for one of those meals. I'm so tired of this bread and cheese.' And he would long for one of those ten course meals. At the end of the journey as he was preparing to go ashore, the captain was waiting to speak to each of the passengers. As the man walked past, the captain stopped him and said, 'I hope you enjoyed the journey.' The man replied that he had enjoyed it very much. 'But,' enquired the captain, 'there is one thing I don't understand. Why didn't you ever come into the dining room and eat with the rest of the people?' The man looked at the captain and said, 'Ah, Captain, if you only knew how much I wanted to, but I couldn't afford it.' The captain said, 'Didn't you know that your meals were included in the price of the ticket?'

The man didn't know what belonged to him. That is what the Body of Christ is like today. The main reason Christians suffer from sickness and poverty is that they lack knowledge of God's Word in those areas. As we gain knowledge we will also gain health and prosperity. Prosperity is the ability to meet any given need at any given time through the power of God. Jesus Christ went to the cross to deliver us from sin, sickness, and spiritual death. We must know what things are guaranteed us through the Word of God. Part of our ticket when we were born again is to be free from all forms of sickness and poverty.

(b) Not acting on the Word of God

Another reason why Christians suffer needlessly is because they do not act on the Word of God.

> Therefore whosoever heareth these sayings of mine, *and doeth them*, I will liken him unto a wise man, which built his house upon a rock: and the rain descended, and the floods came, and the winds blew, and beat upon that house; and it fell not: for it was founded upon a rock. And everyone that heareth these sayings of mine, and doeth them not, shall be likened unto a foolish man, which built his house upon the sand: and the rain descended, and the floods came, and the winds blew, and beat upon that house; and it fell: and great was the fall of it (Matt. 7.24–27, italics mine).

God did not send the floods – they came. The devil will send everything he can along your way. Jesus is saying if you hear His sayings *and do them*, when the floods come (notice He said *when* they come, not *if* they come) you will be victorious. But He also said that if you hear His sayings, and do not do them (notice you can still hear His sayings) when the floods come you will fall. The choice is yours. You can hear the Word of God and not act on it and you will fall.

Many people when they do fall, blame God. The Bible doesn't say that. The Word of God says that when the floods come, it is how you react in the situation that determines whether you stand or fall.

> But be ye doers of the Word, and not hearers only, deceiving your own selves (Jas. 1.22).

If we want the Word of God to benefit us in our lives, we must act on what we hear.

When my Granny was nearly ninety, she went in to the hospital for a check up. The X-rays showed that she had water on the lung. The specialist wanted to admit her into hospital immediately. Granny looked the doctor straight in the eye, and said, 'The only place I'm going is home.' Then she proceeded to tell him how Jesus Christ had died for her sins, and that she was healed by the stripes of

Jesus. And Granny went home totally healed, praise God.

Don't misunderstand me. Doctors are from God, and they are fighting the same enemy as we are. Many times I will pray for a person who is seriously ill, that the doctors will have wisdom in dealing with their case and that their hands will be guided by the Holy Spirit. It depends on the level of faith of the people involved. If a person can believe God for total healing, praise God for it. But, if that is not his level of faith, God will work through doctors.

We must see that God through His Word promises us long life and good health. We can make a choice. My Granny made that choice. Instead of saying that she was old and dying and she might as well go into the hospital and lie there and see her last days, bless God, she said, 'Oh, no, I choose life.' My Granny finally went to be with Jesus when she was ready to go.

That's just what Abraham did, that is how he went to be with the Lord, and Abraham's blessings are mine. So the same choice is mine, and yours.

(c) Opposing the truth

The third reason why Christians suffer is because they oppose the truth. It is very important to have a teachable spirit. When God reveals a truth to you in His Word, even if it doesn't agree with what tradition and religion have taught, be open to what God is saying. Don't have the attitude that says, 'I don't care what the Bible says, I have been doing it this way for the last thirty years.' That type of attitude is opposing the truth.

> So Naaman came with his horses and with his chariot, and stood at the door of the house of Elisha. And Elisha sent a messenger unto him, saying, Go and wash in Jordan seven times, and thy flesh shall come again to thee, and thou shalt be clean. But Naaman was wroth, and went away, and said,

> Behold, I thought, He will surely come out to me, and stand, and call on the name of the Lord his God, and strike his hand over the place, and recover the leper. Are not Abana and Pharpar, rivers of Damascus, better than all the waters of Israel? May I not wash in them, and be clean? So he turned and went away in a rage. And his servants came near, and spake unto him, and said, My father, if the prophet had bid thee do some great thing, wouldest thou not have done it? How much rather then, when he saith to thee, Wash, and be clean? Then went he down, and dipped himself seven times in Jordan, according to the saying of the man of God: and his flesh came again like unto the flesh of a little child, and he was clean (2 Kgs. 5.9–14).

When Naaman first heard the instruction from Elisha, his attitude was in opposition to the truth. He heard what the prophet said, but it wasn't what he thought it should be, so he was prepared to leave without receiving from God. He didn't want to line up with God's Word. He didn't want to line up with what God told him to do through the word of the prophet. Often, that is how we are. We don't want to line up with God's Word. We want it our way. God wants you to do it His way and His way is always the best way. God said through the prophet that Naaman was to wash in the Jordan seven times. If he had washed only once, or even six times, he would not have been healed. But when he dipped himself in the Jordan seven times, he was healed. I don't know why the prophet told him that he needed to dip seven times, all I know is that when he did his skin was made like the flesh of a little child, and he was clean. Had he opposed the truth, he would never have been healed.

Naaman washed seven times, and he was healed.

That is how simple it is. God's Word says it, we believe it, and that settles it.

(d) Living in sin

Many people suffer sickness and other problems because

they live in sin. God desires and commands certain things in the Word of God for our protection.

God does not tell us not to do things because He doesn't like us to have fun. Many people think that God is against fun. He isn't against fun – He is against the things of sin, which look like fun, but will destroy us.

Let's look at it in natural terms. When you were a child and your parents told you to look both ways before crossing the street, did they tell you that for no reason? Did they say it for their sake? No, they would instruct you for your own protection, so that when you crossed the street you would not be run over by a car.

God tells us how to live in order to protect us. It is as if He has an umbrella spread out over His people. On the earth it is raining sickness, sin, poverty, oppression, and every other evil work of the devil. God says if you stay under the umbrella of His protection, by living in obedience to His Word, you will stay free from all of these evil things. But if you go out from under that umbrella, you take yourself out from under God's protection, and it is raining out there.

> Be not deceived; God is not mocked: for whatsoever a man soweth, that shall he also reap. For he that soweth to his flesh shall of the flesh reap corruption; but he that soweth to the spirit, shall of the spirit reap life everlasting (Gal. 6.7–8).

In Galatians 5 we can see what the works of the flesh are: '...adultery, fornication, uncleanness, lasciviousness, idolatry, witchcraft, hatred, variance, emulations, wrath, strife, seditions, heresies, envyings, murders, drunkenness, revellings, and such like.'

Proverbs 6.16 tells of the things which the Lord hates, things that are an abomination to Him: 'a proud look, a lying tongue, and hands that shed innocent blood, an heart that deviseth wicked imaginations, feet that be swift in running to mischief, a false witness that speaketh lies, and he that soweth discord among brethren.'

Sin starts inside the heart and the outward manifestation is the end result. Murder begins in the heart as hatred and then manifests itself outwardly. Pride is listed first in Proverbs 6.16. When people say 'I don't need Jesus. I lead a good life,' that's pride.

Before I committed my life to Jesus, I really 'sowed my wild oats'. And once I began my Christian walk, the devil would keep reminding me of what I had done in the past and telling me that what I had sowed, I would have to reap. But when I came to Jesus, I became a new creature, old things passed away and all things became new (2 Cor. 5.17). The Lord showed me the example of a farmer planting seed. When that seed is planted, it has to be watered and nurtured until it begins to grow. But if the farmer comes back and plucks out the seed, of course it cannot grow. And the way to pluck out that which you have sown once you are a new creature, is to act on 1 John 1.9: 'If we confess our sins, he is faithful and just to forgive us our sins, and to cleanse us from all unrighteousness.'

Many people wonder about unknown sin in their lives. The Word tells us that God will cleanse us from *all* unrighteousness. That is known sin and unknown sin.

> ...but the way of transgressors is hard (Prov. 13.15).

Many times sin can make you sick.

> Is any sick among you? Let him call for the elders of the church; and let them pray over him, anointing him with oil in the name of the Lord. And the prayer of faith shall save the sick, and the Lord shall raise him up; and if he have committed sins, they shall be forgiven him (Jas. 5.14–15).

James is saying that if a person is sick as a result of sin, the prayer of faith can bring healing to him, and his sins will be forgiven. I think most of us have seen the result of a sinful life, where a man lives in such a fashion that it affects his health. You see it often in the world; a film star, married six times, dies at the age of forty. Sin will kill you in the end. The result of sin is death.

> Confess your faults one to another, and pray one for another, that ye may be healed. The effectual fervent prayer of a righteous man availeth much (Jas. 5. 16).

We are not to allow strife to enter in. We are to walk in love and apologise to our brother or sister if we have offended them.

(e) Not discerning the Lord's Body

> Now in this that I declare unto you I praise you not, that ye come together not for the better, but for the worse. For first of all, when ye come together in the church, I hear that there be divisions among you; and I partly believe it. For there must be also heresies among you, that they which are approved may be made manifest among you. When ye come together therefore into one place, this is not to eat the Lord's supper. For in eating every one taketh before other his own supper; and one is hungry and another is drunken. What? have ye not houses to eat and to drink in? or despise ye the church of God, and shame them that have not? What shall I say to you? shall I praise you in this? I praise you not. For I have received of the Lord that which also I delivered unto you, That the Lord Jesus the same night in which he was betrayed took bread: And when he had given thanks, he brake it, and said, Take, eat: this is my body, which is broken for you: this do in remembrance of me. After the same manner also he took the cup, when he had supped, saying, This cup is the new testament in my blood: this do ye, as oft as ye drink it, in remembrance of me. For as often as ye eat this bread, and drink this cup, ye do shew the Lord's death till he come. Wherefore whosoever shall eat this bread, and drink this cup of the Lord, unworthily, shall be guilty of the body and blood of the Lord. But let a man examine himself, and so let him

> eat of that bread, and drink of that cup. For he that eateth and drinketh unworthily, eateth and drinketh damnation to himself, not discerning the Lord's body (1 Cor. 11.17–29).

We need to walk in love towards each other in the Body of Christ.

> For this cause many are weak and sickly among you, and many sleep. For if we would judge ourselves, we should not be judged (1 Cor. 11.30–31).

We need to judge ourselves. And we need to be aware of all that our Lord Jesus Christ has done for us by His sacrifice on the cross, when we partake of communion.

(f) Unforgiveness

Someone says, 'I am believing for my husband to get saved, but when he comes into the same room with me, I feel like hitting him over the head with a stick. But, if God can do anything with him, that's fine.' That person has unforgiveness and bitterness in their heart.

> To whom ye forgive anything, I forgive also, for if I forgave anything, to whom I forgave it, for your sakes I forgave it in the person of Christ; Lest Satan should get an advantage of us: for we are not ignorant of his devices (2 Cor. 2.10–11).

What Paul is saying here is that if we do not walk in forgiveness, we are ignorant of Satan's devices, and he is taking advantage of us. Mark 11.25–26 tells us if we don't forgive as we stand praying, our prayers will not be answered, and the blessings of God cannot flow through us. We ask why our families are apart, and why things are going wrong. It is because we are not walking in love. God is love and God never fails. Therefore love never fails.

(g) Envy and strife

> But if ye have bitter envying and strife in your hearts, glory not, and lie not against the truth. This wisdom descendeth not from above, but is earthly, sensual, devilish. For where envying and strife is, there is confusion and every evil work (Jas. 3.14–16).

When you walk in envy and strife, there will be confusion and every evil work. Often, people say, 'Well, God is allowing this.' No, God has to allow it because you are walking in envy, strife and bitterness.

> And the servant of the Lord must not strive; but be gentle unto all men, apt to teach, patient, in meekness instructing those that oppose themselves; if God peradventure will give them repentance to the acknowledging of the truth; And that they may recover themselves out of the snare of the devil, who are taken captive by him at his will (2 Tim. 2.24–26).

Entering into strife will allow the devil to take you captive at his will.

(h) Pride

> Pride goeth before destruction, and an haughty spirit before a fall (Prov. 16.18).

> ...lest being lifted up with pride, he fall into the condemnation of the devil (1 Tim. 3.6).

Lucifer fell from the heavens because of pride, and he will attempt to cause you to fall by the same means. But, praise God, we can walk before God without pride, in total submission to His will, always ready to share and minister His Word.

(i) Murmuring and complaining

Finally, murmuring and complaining can be a source of suffering.

Neither murmur ye, as some of them also murmured, and were destroyed of the destroyer (1 Cor. 10.10).

Trials and tribulations will come against you. What matters is how you act in them. If you boldly stand on the Word of God and resist the devil, he will flee from you (Jas. 4.7). But if you murmur and complain, you will be destroyed by the destroyer.

5. How God chastises us

Now I want you to understand that you are a spirit, you possess a soul and you live in a body.

And the very God of peace sanctify you wholly; and I pray God your whole spirit and soul and body be preserved blameless unto the coming of our Lord Jesus Christ (1 Thess. 5.23).

For the Word of God is quick and powerful, and sharper than any two-edged sword, piercing even to the dividing asunder of soul and spirit, and of the joints and marrow, and is a discerner of the thoughts and intents of the heart (Heb. 4.12).

You are a spirit. The real you is a spirit being. God is a Spirit and we were created in the image of God.

God is a Spirit: and they that worship him must worship him in spirit and truth (John 4.24).
For as many as are led by the Spirit of God, they are the sons of God (Rom. 8.14).

God communicates with your spirit man which is you.

...the spirit of man is the candle of the Lord...(Prov. 20. 27).

We need to realise that the Spirit of God dwells in our innermost being if we are born again children of God. God communicates with us, He teaches, instructs and corrects us, through our spirit.

(a) Chastisement

The word 'chastisement' means 'guidance, instruction, discipline and correction, as used in training and nurturing a child'.

Now, many people think that the way God chastises a person is through physical pain or illness. I've heard people say that God allowed cancer to come on someone so that two or three in that family could get saved at the funeral!

Fred Price told of a man about thirty-five who was killed in a car accident and his four brothers afterward came to the Lord. Everybody said that showed that it was God's will. Brother Price said, however, that that man was leading four or five people a week to the Lord. If he had lived another thirty-five years, just think how many more he could have won to the Lord.

We need to see that Jesus came to give us abundant life (John 10.10). He said that the devil comes to steal, kill and destroy, but He (Jesus) came that we might have life and life more abundantly. *More* abundantly, not less abundantly.

> As many as I love, I rebuke and chasten: be zealous therefore, and repent (Rev. 3.19).

In other words Jesus is saying that as many as He loves, He corrects and guides and instructs and disciplines.

> ...the goodness of God leadeth thee to repentance (Rom. 2.4).

The goodness of God leadeth thee to repentance. When we begin to see the goodness of God, we want to serve Him because we love Him. Not from fear and not because He will punish us one day if we don't. *God is love* therefore *love is God*.

Many times when people read in the Bible that God will chastise us, they say, 'Here we go again, God is going to chastise me and if He makes me ill, I'll just take it because He is trying to teach me something.'

Could a loving earthly father possibly desire to give his child cancer in order to teach him something? Surely our Heavenly Father loves us even more. We need to understand that we have a father son relationship with God.

> Ye have not yet resisted unto blood, striving against sin. And ye have forgotten the exhortation which speaketh unto you as unto children, My son, despise not thou the chastening of the Lord, nor faint when thou art rebuked of him (Heb. 12.4–5).

We need to have a teachable spirit so that God can speak to us.

Oh, I have been rebuked by the Lord when I have missed it or been disobedient to the Word. I've known I've done something which has grieved the Spirit of God, and it has twisted me inside. I have known that I need to put it right immediately. If we do not listen to the Spirit of God – if we are not sensitive to the Spirit of God – if we cannot be corrected by the Word of God, what happens is that we get out from under the protection of God. Then the devil will make sure that he attacks us in every way possible. After that, perhaps, we will get back to the Word. But the Word was there *before* the devil attacked us.

However, people will stand up and testify, 'Bless God, I was in a car accident, had five broken ribs, two broken arms, etc. etc.' and give the devil the glory for half an hour. Then for about five seconds, they will say '...and out of all that I found Jesus.' They could have found Jesus before the car accident. The Word of God was there before the accident!

> For whom the Lord loveth, he chasteneth [corrects, instructs, disciplines, guides] (Heb. 12.6).

God does that for our benefit and not His. Many people think that God tells us to live according to the Word of God because He enjoys seeing us do that. No, He tells us these things in the Word of God – His Manual of Life – for our benefit.

There is no sickness or poverty in heaven.

Let me paraphrase Hebrews 12.7–9:

> If ye endure correction, instruction, discipline, guidance, God dealeth with you as with sons. [This is the father son relationship.] For what son is he whom the father does not correct, instruct, discipline or guide? But if ye be without guidance, correction, discipline or instruction, then are ye bastards and not sons. Furthermore, we have had fathers of our flesh which corrected us, and we gave them reverence: shall we not much rather be in subjection unto the Father of spirits, and live?

Let us read verse 9 from the Amplified Bible:

> Moreover, we have had earthly fathers who disciplined us and we yielded to them and respected them for training us. Shall we not much more cheerfully submit to the Father of spirits, and so truly live?

You have not experienced the fullness and power of God until you are walking in His Word. Now verse 11:

> Now no chastening for the present seemeth to be joyous, but grievous: nevertheless afterward it yieldeth the peaceable fruit of righteousness unto them which are exercised thereby.

Sometimes I read the Word and the Spirit of the Lord will come up on the inside of me and say, 'You had better make it right with that person.'

And I will say, 'Dear Lord, anything else – I'll scrub the floor, I'll sing twelve choruses a day, anything but that.'

'No,' the Lord will say, 'you have to go and tell him, "Brother, I love you with the love of the Lord, and I love you myself."'

It's not enough just to say, 'I love you with the love of the Lord' – we need to love them ourselves as well! The minute I go and straighten that thing out, the minute I am obedient to my spirit, the blessings of God begin to flow in my life. At times, the person whom I think will begin to laugh at me when I say I'm sorry, will begin to weep instead and say, 'I can see God this morning working in your life.' God always knows what He is doing.

Let us now read Hebrews 12.5–11 from the Amplified Bible:

> And have you (completely) forgotten the divine word of appeal and encouragement in which you are reasoned with and addressed as sons? My son, do not think lightly or scorn to submit to the correction and discipline of the Lord, nor lose courage and give up and faint when you are reproved or corrected by Him;
>
> For the Lord corrects and disciplines every one whom He loves, and He punishes, even scourges, every son whom He accepts and welcomes to His heart and cherishes.
>
> You must submit to and endure (correction) for discipline. God is dealing with you as with sons; for what son is there whom his father does not (thus) train and correct and discipline?
>
> Now if you are exempt from correction and left without discipline in which all (of God's children) share, then you are illegitimate offspring and not true sons (at all).
>
> Moreover, we have had earthly fathers who disciplined us and we yielded (to them) and respected (them for training us). Shall we not much more cheerfully submit to the Father of spirits and so (truly) live?
>
> For (our earthly fathers) disciplined us for only a short period of time and chastised us as seemed proper and good to them, but He disciplines us for our certain good, that we may become sharers in His own holiness.
>
> For the time being no discipline brings joy but seems grievous and painful, but afterwards it yields peaceable fruit of righteousness to those who have been trained by it – a harvest of fruit

which consists in righteousness (that is, in conformity to God's will in purpose, thought and action, resulting in right living and right standing with God).

Every part of your being will be in right standing with God when the Spirit of God leads you.

> All scripture is given by inspiration of God, and is profitable for doctrine, for reproof, for correction, for instruction in righteousness (2 Tim. 3.16).

God disciplines us through His Word.

6. Do we thank God for everything?

Should we thank God for everything that happens in our lives? Do we have to thank Him for all the wars of the world? Do we have to thank Him when we lose a loved one or when sickness comes our way? To find the answers to these questions, we need to study the Scriptures.

> Study to shew thyself approved unto God, a workman that needeth not to be ashamed, rightly dividing the word of truth (2 Tim. 2.15).

The Bible is consistent from Genesis to Revelation – it does not contradict itself as some people think, and we need to rightly divide the word of truth.

> And whatsoever ye do in word or deed do all in the name of the Lord Jesus, giving thanks to God and the Father by him (Col. 3.17).

Does that mean that the war in Ireland is God's will, because people say it is being fought in the name of Christianity? The Crusaders acted in the name of Christianity when they beheaded people if they refused to be baptised. This is what brought about the Dark Ages – when witchcraft and other demonic activities were allowed to develop in the Church – all in the name of Christianity. That is why many people say, 'If that is Christianity, I don't want any part of it.'

Do we thank God for all that because it was done in the name of Jesus Christ? *No, we need to rightly divide the Word of truth.*

> Giving thanks always for all things unto God and the Father in the name of our Lord Jesus Christ (Eph. 5.20).

At first glance it seems that this verse is saying that we need to give thanks always for all things, even tragedy or hardship, even when a child is run over by a car; we are to thank God for it. But let's look at a natural father son relationship. If a father deliberately injures or kills his child, he is punished by law – everyone agrees that the father has done a wicked thing. Yet people will blame our Father God for something that even an earthly father would not do to his child. We only need to watch a loving father with his child to see that he could not possibly desire to injure him – and he is just an earthly imperfect man. Surely our Father God loves us even more and would never deliberately make us ill or take our lives from us.

Let us examine Ephesians 5.20 again:

> Giving thanks always for all things unto God.

All things unto God – Don't give thanks for things that are not unto God. Give thanks to God for the things of God, and blame the devil for the things of the devil. We don't thank God for what the devil is doing.

Jesus Himself told us this in Matthew 22.16–21:

> And they sent out unto him their disciples with the Herodians, saying, Master, we know that thou art true, and teachest the way of God in truth, neither carest thou for any man: for thou regar-

dest not the person of men.

Tell us therefore, What thinkest thou? Is it lawful to give tribute unto Caesar, or not?

But Jesus perceived their wickedness, and said, Why tempt ye me, ye hypocrites? Shew me the tribute money. And they brought unto him a penny. And he saith unto them, Whose is this image and superscription?

They say unto him, Caesar's. Then saith he unto them, Render therefore unto Caesar the things which are Caesar's; and unto God the things that are God's.

Jesus is saying, 'Give Caesar what belongs to Caesar and give God what belongs to God. Attribute to the devil the things that are the devil's and give God the things that are God's.' But people get confused about what is of the devil and what is of God.

Jesus never praised God for the works of the devil. While the storm was beating against the boat crossing the sea of Galilee, He didn't say, 'Let's thank God for the storm.'

When the ten lepers came to Jesus, He didn't say, 'Let's thank God for the leprosy.' He simply spoke to the storm and stilled it, and He reached out and healed the lepers.

Jesus said, 'I have come that you might have life and life more abundantly, the devil comes to steal, kill and destroy.'

When Jesus raised Lazarus from the dead, He didn't thank God for the fact that Lazarus was dead, He thanked God that His prayers were always heard; then He spoke to Lazarus and told him to come forth.

Jesus never thanked God for what the devil did.

> For this purpose the Son of God was manifested, that he might destroy the works of the devil (1 John 3.8).

Some people act as if God and the devil are working together. They say that God is sending the devil; as if God and the devil have fellowship together and discuss how they are going to attack someone!

But the Bible says that we are to resist the devil and he will flee from us because Jesus has already defeated him. Jesus has given us the armour of God, His name and the Holy Spirit – we have to live by the rules that God has set out for us in His Word. Jesus is not going to resist the devil again for us. We now have to resist him in the name of Jesus and he will flee from us (Jas. 4.7).

> In everything give thanks: for this is the will of God in Christ Jesus concerning you (1 Thess. 5.18).

This verse does not say, 'Thank God *for* everything' but 'Thank God *in* everything.' There is a big difference between giving thanks for a situation and giving thanks in a situation. I will not thank the devil *for* what he is doing in my life, but *in* the situation, I will give thanks unto God. I can give thanks to God in any situation knowing that I have victory over sickness because:

> ...by his stripes I have been healed (1 Pet. 2.24).

> ...himself took our infirmities, and bare our sicknesses (Matt. 8. 17).

> Who healeth all thy diseases (Ps. 103.3).

I have victory over financial problems because:

> But my God shall supply all your need according to his riches in glory by Christ Jesus (Phil. 4.19).

> Who hath blessed us with all spiritual blessings in heavenly places in Christ (Eph. 1.3).

> Beloved, I wish above all things that thou mayest prosper and be in health, even as thy soul prospereth (3 John 2).

> ...and whatsoever he doeth shall prosper (Ps. 1.3).

Therefore I can rejoice always and praise God in every situation. No matter what test or trial comes our way, God will always provide a way of escape.

> There is no temptation taken you but such as is common to man: but *God is faithful*, who will not suffer you to be tempted above that ye are able; but will with the temptation also make a way to escape, that ye may be able to bear it (1 Cor. 10.13).

How can we believe that God puts us into trials and temptations and then while He has us there, gives us a way out? God doesn't work that way – the trials and temptations come from the devil and God gives us a way of escape through His Word.

One might ask, why does God allow these trials and temptations to come our way? Why did God allow Adam to sin? Why did God allow Judas to betray Jesus? Why did God allow Paul to persecute Christians? Why does God allow people to die, and go to hell when the Bible tells us that He is not willing that any should perish?

Why? The answer is simple. There is something that separates us from every other living creature – our will. Our will is sovereign. The word 'sovereign' means 'supreme power' – your will is the supreme power in your life. You can be saved, Spirit filled and still go and rob a bank; God won't stop you. If you want to be sick, God will allow it because your will is sovereign.

Satan is the god of this world (2 Cor. 4.4) but God tells us that we have a choice.

> I call heaven and earth to record this day against you, that I have set before you life and death; blessing and cursing: therefore choose life, that both thou and thy seed may live (Deut. 30.19).

Jesus came to give us abundant life. He said:

> The Spirit of the Lord is upon me, because he hath anointed me to preach the gospel to the poor; he hath sent me to heal the brokenhearted, to preach deliverance to the captives, and recovering of sight to the blind, to set at liberty them that are bruised, to preach the acceptable year of the Lord (Luke 4.18–19).

> Offer unto God thanksgiving; and pay thy vows unto the most High: And call upon me in the day of trouble: I will deliver thee, and thou shalt glorify me (Ps. 50.14–15).

When we begin to praise and worship God – when we begin to give Him all the glory, then He will deliver us from all our troubles.

6

God's total protection: deliverance and rewards

As we have seen, one of the biggest problems in these last days is that people do not know who is doing what to whom. They blame God for things that have nothing to do with Him. If you think that it is God who is making you sick, persecuting and oppressing you to teach you a lesson, then there is no way that you can resist it in the name of Jesus. So let us find out in more detail who our enemy is and who God is.

There is a clause in insurance policies describing disasters as acts of God, as if God is the one who is destroying people. Jesus said, 'I am come that they [the sheep] might have life, and that they might have it more abundantly' (John 10.10). The devil (the thief) 'cometh not, but to steal, and to kill, and to destroy'. That is the one that destroys and I served him for twenty-four years before I became born again. The God that I serve now is not out to destroy everything; He is a rewarder, not a destroyer; He is in the adding-unto business, not the taking away; He is a deliverer, not an oppressor.

> But without faith it is impossible to please him: for he that cometh to God must believe that he is, and that he is a rewarder of them that diligently seek him (Heb. 11.6).

1. Deliverance from deceit

Let us look again at Psalm 91 to see what deliverance and rewards are promised to us in God's Word (see also p. 132 in section 7 of chapter 3).

> Surely he shall deliver thee from the snare of the fowler (Ps. 91.3).

The Word promises that God shall deliver you from the traps, the devices, that the hunter will lay across your path. Who hunts you? Surely not God, but the enemy, the devil.

(a) Deceitful doctrine

> Now the Spirit speaketh expressly, that in the latter times some shall depart from the faith, giving heed to seducing spirits, and doctrines of devils; Speaking lies in hypocrisy; having their conscience seared with a hot iron; Forbidding to marry, and commanding to abstain from meats, which God hath created to be received with thanksgiving of them which believe and know the truth (1 Tim. 4.1–3).

(b) Deceitful teaching on God's Word

Many people today are being deceived concerning God's Word. People are told that the signs and wonders and the outpouring of the Spirit, as it happened in the book of Acts, have passed away, that things like that do not happen today any more. They are being told that the Word of God is not really true and I have heard ministers turn around and say that you cannot really believe the Word of God in these last days and that it does not mean what it says. Well, I am simple enough to believe the Bible, and if it does not mean what it says, then I wish God would have said what He really meant.

God's Word has been watered down for long enough; it is time for us to rectify it and the best way to do it is to look at what Jesus told the apostles to do in Mark 16.15–20. They were simple enough to follow His instructions; they applied it just as He told them to do, and we read in the book of Acts of the signs and wonders that followed them, just as Jesus promised them. Do you want the Lord working with you, and confirming His Word with signs following? Do you want to be able in the name of Jesus to cast out devils, let blind eyes recover their sight, make deaf ears hear, raise up the sick and even the dead? Well, I believe with all my heart that the book of Acts is the blueprint for the Church today. Miracles should be just as much a part of our ministry as the Body of Christ today, as they were in the book of Acts. Jesus said, 'He that believeth on me, the works that I do shall he do also; and greater works than these shall he do; because I go unto my Father' (John 14.12). I believe that that is still true for the ministry of the believer in these last days; I believe that Jesus Christ is exactly the same as He has always been.

> Jesus Christ the same yesterday, and today, and for ever (Heb. 13.8).

> For I am the Lord, I change not (Mal. 3.6).

(c) Deceitful teaching on other religions

Another expression that we find today is that all roads lead to Rome. People often use it to mean that as long as you believe in some god, never mind what you call him – Buddha, Allah, Muhammed or whatever – you will get eternal life. Just lead a good life, they say. Well, it is not true. If everybody should leave their homes right now, and just take any old road, leading in any direction, they would not all get to Rome. The Bible teaches us what the correct way to heaven is: Jesus. He said: 'I am the way, the truth, and the life: no man cometh unto the Father, but by me' (John 14.6).

That is my final authority: the Word of God says it; that

settles it; I believe it. If we believe in His Word, and keep the conditions, He will deliver us from the snare of the fowler.

2. Deliverance from disease

Secondly He will deliver you 'from the noisome pestilence'. The word 'pestilence' means infectious or contagious or a deadly disease. So the Word of God declares that He delivers us from infectious or contagious or deadly diseases. As I was studying this the Lord told me: 'I want you to pray for the incurable diseases, because I am going to make them curable.' When there is no hope with man, there is always hope in God.

In one of the books by John G. Lake, I read that he had ten thousand people healed through a healing clinic that he had in America. Ten thousand people! God is still in the miracle-working business. God is not asleep, and God has not disappeared. He is still around. He is well and alive on Planet Earth.

3. Deliverance from fear

The third thing that He delivered us from is 'terror by night' (Ps. 91.5). People have been conditioned not even to go out at night. There is so much terror around in the world that people are too terrified to go out of their apartments. I went to pray for a man one day and he was too terrified to leave his apartment. The more stories you hear about rape, about muggings and other crimes, and the more you feed your spirit on these things, looking at it on television and films, the more terrified you get. However, the Bible declares that we do not have to be scared of the terror at night, because the Greater One indwells us.

If you were sitting in your room at night and your lights were off and Jesus came in and sat down next to you, would you be scared of the dark? You see, you have got Jesus living inside you, so how can you be scared of the dark? When I was a little boy, I would wake up in my bedroom in the middle of the night in the dark and I would really be scared. I used to run out of my room to my daddy's bedroom, wake him up and jump into his bed. He would pacify me and take me back, and as he walked into that room with me, I would not be scared any more, because I had my big daddy with me. Well, we have the Greater One, we have the Holy Spirit in us, walking with us into every situation of our lives, so we should not be scared of anything. Besides that, you have the name of Jesus to use as a weapon. Every believer has the right to use the name of Jesus and you will be surprised at what will happen when you have the name of Jesus and the Greater One in you. Jesus said:

> Hitherto have ye asked nothing in my name: ask, and ye shall receive, that your joy may be full (John 16.24).

Sometimes people ask me to pray for them for more power in their lives. My reply invariably has been: 'You have the Father, Son and Holy Spirit living in you; how much more power do you want?'

Terry Mize spent a lot of time doing missionary work in Mexico, and in his book *More Than Conquerors*, he tells this true story. He was driving in his car and noticed a hitchhiker at the side of the road. He stopped his car to give the man a lift. When the man was inside Terry's car, he pulled out a gun and commanded Terry to hand over everything he owned. Terry said: 'You cannot steal anything from me. In the name of Jesus I will give it to you willingly, but there is no way you can steal it.'

The man forced Terry to stop the car and then he told Terry that not only was he going to steal everything that Terry owned, but he was going to kill Terry as well. Terry kept on saying: 'You cannot steal anything from me: I will give it to you and in the name of Jesus, you cannot kill me.' The man pulled the trigger and from six to eight feet away, he fired at Terry five times. Now that is point-blank range.

'If I cannot kill you,' the man said, 'I am going to tie you up naked to a tree and you can stay there and die.' Terry held on to his confession and told the man again that he could not do anything to him. The man tied him to the tree and walked off, but returned and untied him, gave him back his clothes and got into the car with him. Terry led him to Jesus Christ right there and then. Afterwards Terry found out that the man was wanted for murders. What a testimony! Your angels are encamped around you to protect you.

One day, while I was alone in the house, taking a shower and praising God, I became aware of a being standing next to me. Now, I could not see him with my physical eye, but the anointing of God just came over me and I knew that my personal angel who looks after me was there. I got onto my knees right there in my shower and began to praise God.

If you really know that your angels are there, right with you, you are ready to take on the world. An angel is not a bold little baby, that looks like a tiny dwarf; a chubby little thing, a little bumble-bee with fancy wings and a tiny bow and arrow. No, I would not want angels like that to protect me, would you? Are you trying to tell me that a little dwarf, a fat little baby with a little dinky bow and arrow will keep back armies? The angel of the Lord in 2 Kings 19.35 struck and killed 185,000 soldiers in one night in the camp of the Assyrians – that does not sound like the work of a little fat baby to me. If you read up about angels, their ministry, and people that they appeared to, you will find out for yourselves that they are mighty beings. The Bible says in the book of Hebrews that they are spirits sent forth to minister to you. Wherever I go, I send my ministering angels before me and they do a good job. Hallelujah.

4. Deliverance from harm

Fourthly, He will deliver you from 'the arrow that flieth by day'. God will protect you from bullets, riots, wars and attackers. I want to quote something from a book called *Hand on the Helm* by Catherine Carter. This is a historically true and confirmed incident.

> For four long years, in the frontline warfare of World War I, a British regiment did not have one casualty. They did not lose a single man. They could only give one explanation for this incredible record. During those interminable years of danger and valour, every officer and every enlisted man in the regiment daily affirmed his faith in God's protection by repeating the 91st Psalm.

The book goes on to say that each officer and soldier in the regiment carried a complete copy of the Psalm and either read it or recited it from memory daily.

> Considering the casualty totals for the war, and, more specifically, considering the casualties experienced by adjacent regiments, the chances that an entire regiment could go through such frontline battles without a single casualty, were astronomical. Religious magazines on both sides of the Atlantic published the story and it was pointed out, as hard as it might be for some people to believe that bullets and shells, aimed at the men of this regiment, were supernaturally deflected it was still harder to believe that coincidence could have sent that many bullets astray.

I think that the Minister of Defence should get every person on active duty to carry Psalm 91.

5. Deliverance from floods and earthquakes

God also delivers us from 'the destruction that wasteth at noonday'. Now, I might stand on a few toes, but God spoke to me specifically about these words and He answered a few of my questions. Destruction at noonday refers to floods and earthquakes. Many people blame God for floods. I will never forget that a while ago, when they had a flood in South Africa, somebody said on a television broadcast that God was punishing that specific town. Now the Lord spoke to me and said: 'Am I a respecter of persons?' After I said 'No', He said: 'Did I not tell Abraham that if they had ten righteous people in Sodom and Gomorrah, I would not destroy it? Are there not more than ten righteous people in South Africa?' Praise God. God is not going to pour His wrath out on His Church. God's wrath will be poured out on the earth after we leave it; after the rapture, but not before.

I want to ask you another question: how many revivals have ever come because of a flood? When Mel Tari and a few other people in Indonesia raised someone from the dead three days after he died, 350,000 people got saved. That is what brings revival: miracles, signs and wonders lead to revival, not disasters. The goodness of God leads to repentance.

If you are serving God because you are scared of Him, you are serving the wrong person. God is a good God and He is going to protect us. There are a lot of prophets of doom going around saying that South Africa is finished, Britain is finished, the world is finished. I have news for them: while the Body of Christ is here, the world is not finished: we still have work to do for the kingdom of God and He will protect us so that we can get it done on time. After the rapture the old earth will be finished and will pass away, so that a new heaven and a new earth will be created.

Now I want to explain the rewards that you can enjoy if you meet the conditions for God's total protection in Psalm 91.

6. God's reward: his Word for a shield

His truth is His Word. You have the Word of God that is sharper than a two-edged sword. Have you ever taken your Bible and used it as a sword to fight the devil? Jesus used it.

He used the Word of God as His shield. Remember when He was in the wilderness and the devil came to Him? He said: 'It is written....' If Jesus had to use the Word of God as a shield, who do you think you are that you do not have to do it? If it was good enough for Jesus and if He had to speak the Word to get things done, then surely we have to do the same to get results: resist the devil and he will flee from you.

7. God's reward: release

The second reward is in verse five: 'thou shalt not be afraid...' 2 Timothy 1.7 says that God has not given us a spirit of fear. If you are in fear tonight, it is not from God. God has not given us a spirit of fear, but of love and a sound mind.

God has said 366 times in the Bible: 'Fear not' – once for every day of the year. I think He is trying to tell us something, don't you? Jesus has done the work 2,000 years ago. He redeemed us from sin, sickness and poverty by dying on the cross. Galatians 3.13 tells us: 'Christ hath redeemed us from the curse of the law, being made a curse for us: for it is written, Cursed is every one that hangeth on a tree.'

The Amplified Bible says: 'Christ purchased our freedom redeeming us...' 'Redeem' is defined in the dictionary as 'buy back, recover by expenditure of effort or by stipulated payment'. Surely He paid the stipulated payment to buy us back from all the curses of the law as it is set out in Deuteronomy 28.15–67. He did it for every born-again believer, but it is up to you to receive it. I do not care who you are, Jesus went to the cross to redeem you, whether you believe it or not: He has redeemed you; it is up to you to receive it and to believe it.

> When thou passest through the waters, I will be with thee; and through the rivers, they shall not overflow thee: when thou walkest through the fire, thou shalt not be burned; neither shall the

flame kindle upon thee. For I am the Lord thy God, the Holy One of Israel, thy Saviour (Isa. 43.2–3).

When the devil comes against you, just stand on the Word of God: confess it and believe it; do it over and over and tell the devil that the fight is not over until you have won and beaten him. God promises you in His Word that He will be with you, He will protect you in every situation. When you speak the Word of God you have a light that is like a fire; when the devil brings a bucket of water to put it out, you should make steam out of it. Unfortunately, most of us, instead of turning the water into steampower, go up in a puff of smoke: some of us are smoky Christians.

Only with thine eyes shalt thou behold and see the reward of the wicked (Ps. 91.8).

People in the world look at us and think: 'What a bunch of clowns on a Sunday night in that church.' I mean, here I am dancing before the Lord as if I am doing the latest funky chicken dance-step. Some young girls came to Norval Hayes one night and told him that whenever they go to the disco, his daughter is always first on the floor, doing the funky chicken. He said: 'Don't worry about it, I bound the devil in her life and Jesus is going to funky her chicken, don't worry.' Do you know what he did? For two years he stood by the window every time that she went out and he would say: 'Devil, you will not have my daughter. Devil, you will not have my daughter; you have no authority over her, in the name of Jesus.'

He did that for two solid years and one night, quite late, she came out of her room, shaking and as white as a sheet. She said: 'Dad, a big angel came to visit me.' From that day she was not funky any more; she repented, Hallelujah.

Some people think that we are missing all the fun, but I want to tell you that five minutes with the anointing of God in your life is worth a million years elsewhere. I know, for I spent five years working in a nightclub, and I saw the fun they had there. The Bible says the reward of sin is death. Sin will destroy you. It will destroy your family, your relationship with your wife and your health. You can have as much money as you like, as much power as you like; if you are living in sin it will destroy you one way or another. You will either die a very sick man with a lot of money or a very lonely man and you will still finish up with nothing afterwards.

In our church we have some of the best-looking young girls in Johannesburg and they all love Jesus. They used to go to some of the suburbs in Johannesburg and tell the young men that they would meet them at the Constantia cinema at such and such a time. The young men used to think: 'Ah, great! Movies, we'll be there!' The men did not know at the time that we were using the cinema as a church and a considerable number of them came and were saved in this way.

One night, when Sandy Brown was preaching, a drug addict was brought in. During the sermon we heard a big noise and we saw a man on the floor. It was the drug addict. God had knocked him clean off his feet, he hit his head against the wall, but when he got up he shouted: 'I am delivered, and set free. I am healed, I am free.'

When Jesus shines through a woman, and when the love of God is flowing through a woman or a man, they radiate beauty and love and joy. That was one of the things that brought me to Jesus. I walked into a gathering one night while I was still working in a nightclub as a bouncer, and I thought: 'What's going on here?' People were singing, clapping their hands, smiling and I thought they were the funniest people that I had ever seen in my life. But after about thirty minutes I thought: 'Wait a minute, these people have got something that I've been looking for. I've trained my body in a gymnasium for six hours every day and have done everything I know to achieve success in that field, but these people have got what we really should be looking for.' Well, that night I found it: I found Jesus and He changed my life.

God is moving on all kinds of people in these last days. You are going to find bodybuilders, sportsmen, actors, engineers coming to Jesus; because He alone has got the answer, and we have the joy. You cannot buy the peace and joy of Jesus Christ; there is just no way of purchasing it: you receive it by grace after you have accepted Him as Lord of your life.

8. God's reward: answered prayer

> I will answer him: I will be with him in trouble; I will deliver him, and honour him (Ps. 91.15).

Is it not a wonderful thing to know that when you ask whatsoever you desire, and believe that you will get it, you will receive it? One of the rewards is that God will answer you. God desires to do everything in His power to answer your prayers. God is not the one who is hindering your prayers; if you are not getting answers, the problem is with you, not with God.

9. God's reward: honour

Psalm 91.15 also tells us that God will honour us. Isn't that a beautiful promise? Have you ever taken the Scripture and meditated on it? The Most High God will honour you – what a reward! If you walk and talk in line with God's Word, He will honour you. He will honour what you say and what you do, because He will always honour His Word and will never go against it. That shows us the love of God.

10. God's reward: a long and satisfying life

Verse 16 of Psalm 91 gives us another promise of a beautiful reward: 'With long life will I satisfy him, and shew him my salvation.' There is a two-fold promise in the first part of that verse: not only will He give us long life, but He will also satisfy us. To be satisfied certainly does not mean that you should be moaning and complaining all day long: God wants to *satisfy* you with long life. He does not want you to live a long, unhappy and suffering life. He wants you to be satisfied and satisfaction could be yours today in Jesus Christ: you just have to believe it and receive it.

The verse also tells us that He will show us His salvation. The word 'salvation' means to be made whole, to be made complete. Not only is there redemption of sin in salvation, but there is redemption from unrest and there is peace in the plan of redemption. When you accept Jesus as your Lord and Saviour, He sets you free from sin, from poverty, spiritual death and sickness. It is all provided for you in the plan of salvation when you come to Jesus Christ.

7

God's willingness to answer prayer

Let us look at the subject of prayer, and specifically at what Jesus said about prayer. It is important to know what Jesus said about prayer, because He is our example, and I want to show you that Jesus revealed God's character in prayer. In His prayer life and in what He said about prayer, He revealed the willingness of God to answer prayer.

The problems with prayer are on the receiving end – our end – and not on the giving end – God's end. If we knew how to pray according to the spiritual rules that are explained in God's Word; if we had the knowledge to pray correctly in every specific situation, our results would be a hundred per cent better. The problem is not with God. I learned long ago that if things are not working the way that the Bible says they should work, you must look to yourself to find the problem, and not blame God.

> Ask, and it shall be given you; seek, and ye shall find; knock, and it shall be opened unto you: For everyone that asketh receiveth; and he that seeketh findeth; and to him that knocketh it shall be opened. Or what man is there of you, whom if his son ask bread, will he give him a stone? Or if he ask a fish, will he give him a serpent? If ye then, being evil, know how to give good gifts unto your children, how much more shall your Father which is in heaven give good things to them that ask him? (Matt. 7.7–11).

If a person is seeking to find the truth, he will find it: that is what Jesus said. God is not the one who is hindering your prayer life, you are. You have to get to know the character of God; Jesus shook the religious people of His day when He started praying: 'Daddy, Abba, Father, who art in heaven....' He never even said: 'My Father who is in heaven....' He said: 'Our Father....' You need to realise and get to know the attributes and characteristics of God, the Father, towards us, His children. (See chapter 1, The Character of God.) When you become a child of God you automatically qualify for all of God's parenthood towards you.

Jesus said that God is a good Father and will give good things to them that ask Him. So take the good things and place them under what God will give you and place the bad things under the gifts from the devil. God is not concerned about things, He is concerned about your heart; He will give you whatever you want, as long as your heart is right and as long as you are serving Him in the right way. God is not sitting up there and saying: 'Well, Ray, I want to tell you, Fred Roberts was up here ten minutes before you, and I gave everything I had to him, I cannot help you, I have nothing left.' With your children, you are concerned with their motives and attitudes and the way they are living, rather than how much they have: it is the same with God.

Some people say that you must be careful when you pray for the Holy Spirit, because you can receive the wrong spirit; you had better be careful because you might pick up the devil's tongue, they say. They have called it all sorts of things: a foul spirit tongue, the wrong tongue, the other tongue, even calling it a Kenneth Hagin spirit. Because of this, many people who come up when we give an altar call for people to be baptised in the Holy Spirit, are so scared that they will get something that is not the Holy Spirit, that they are too scared to open their mouths and to speak in a new tongue. Let us see what Jesus said about it in the Gospel of Luke, chapter eleven:

> If a son shall ask bread of any of you that is a father, will he give him a stone? or if he ask a fish, will he for a fish give him a serpent? Or if he shall ask an egg, will he offer him a scorpion? If ye then, being evil, know how to give good gifts unto your children: how much more shall your heavenly Father give the Holy Spirit to them that ask him? (Luke 11:11–13).

The baptism of the Holy Spirit with the evidence of speaking in other tongues is a gift, something that you cannot earn; so if you come before God and you ask Him to baptise you and to fill you with the Holy Spirit, that is exactly what you are going to get: no more and no less.

God wants you to have results in your prayer life, never mind what tradition says. Let us look at what John writes:

> And in that day ye shall ask me nothing. Verily, verily, I say unto you, Whatsoever ye shall ask the Father in my name, he will give it you. Hitherto have ye asked nothing in my name: ask, and ye shall receive, that your joy may be full (John 16.23–24).

He did not say '... that *my* joy will be full...' but '... that *your* joy may be full'. You can have a lot of joy, being a Christian; God is not against you having a lot of joy: the Bible teaches us that the joy of the Lord should be your strength. You can live for Jesus a hundred per cent and have a great time; you can even have a sense of humour.

All you have to do to get God's attention, is to use the name of Jesus.

> And it shall come to pass, that before they call, I will answer; and while they are yet speaking, I will hear (Isa. 65.24).

> Now unto him that is able to do exceeding abundantly above all that we ask or think, according to the power that worketh in us, unto him be glory... (Eph. 3.20–21).

That certainly tells us that God wants to answer our prayers and make us prosper.

There are conditions set out in God's Word that are applicable to our prayer life. Conditions 1 and 2 are that you should be obedient and that you should be willing. Isaiah 1.19 says that to eat the good of the land you must be obedient and willing. Not just one or the other; but both together.

Condition 3 is found in the scripture that we quoted above, Ephesians 3.20. It tells us that He is able to do exceeding abundantly above what we ask or think according to – that is a condition – according to the power that worketh in us. There must not only be a power in us, it should also work in us. This condition, like all the conditions in the Bible, will always apply. In other words, if the power of God is doing nothing in you, then you will get nothing.

Nothing is impossible to him who believes. We have so much power in us that, if we can get tapped into it, to release it, we are going to see many more miraculous things happening: exceeding abundantly above all that we ask or think; but we will have to know how to pray.

Many of us have prayed for people, maybe a loved one or family member, to get saved; however, we do not always see results. How should we then go about it? We should see what Jesus told us to do and stick to what He said; to what He taught us to do, and not to what we think He told us to do.

Many of us have prayed: 'Oh, God, please save my aunt and uncle.' Or 'Jesus, please save Mrs Smith,' and so on. Did you know that Jesus never told us to pray that way?

Let me first ask you this question: do you believe that it is God's will and desire to save everybody? Yes, we know from the Bible that it is; well then the problem is not with God saving them, the problem is with us: we are not praying in the right way so that He can get into a position to get them saved.

2 Corinthians 4.4 tells us that Satan is the god of this world, that he has a lease on this earth. The fullness of the earth belonged to God. God gave it to Adam and Adam gave it over to the devil, who now has a lease on it. Now, that should answer ninety per cent of the questions people ask about God killing animals in floods everywhere. It is not God who does that: God is a good God, He does good things.

If God could just save everybody and if He could do the job Himself tonight, then we could all relax and go home to be with Him. God is waiting to send His Son to take us back home with Him, because He is waiting for us to get people saved.

Some people think that the reason we are here is to be taught the Word of God so that we can grow to maturity: yes, God wants us to grow and get more mature in His Word so that we can go into the world and bring others into the kingdom. The more mature and powerful you get in the Spirit of God, the more effectual the tool you are going to be for Him. That is why we are to be taught and to get to the place where we can walk in the Spirit, be victorious, be world-overcomers, so that we can preach the gospel to every creature and to get them into a position to be saved. The purpose of our earthly lives is to get people saved.

My wife, Lindie, and I prayed the wrong way for many years, but, after one month of praying the correct way, according to the Word of God, my brother-in-law and sister-in-law got saved. Kenneth Hagin prayed for fifteen years for one of his relations and, three days after Jesus showed him where to go in God's Word and how to pray, that person was saved.

We have to learn what Jesus said, because what He said, He said for a reason; He did not play with words, He used them. He knew that the Gospels were going to be written by Matthew, Mark, Luke and John; He knew that every word He said was going to be recorded for us to use as a way to live, so He would not say anything unnecessarily. He meant what He said: He did not give you an option. He showed you the right way.

> And Jesus went about all the cities and villages, teaching in their synagogues, and preaching the gospel of the kingdom, and healing every sickness and every disease among the people.
>
> But when he saw the multitudes, he was moved with compassion on them (Matt. 9.35–36).

He is the same today as He was yesterday; God's heartbeat is the same today as when Jesus walked the earth. His heartbeat is for the lost multitudes, and we are the Body of Christ on the earth today. Angels cannot preach the gospel, it is up to us to do it. We need to be filled with compassion when we see people who are lost; and how can they believe unless they have heard? How can they hear unless you tell them? Do not judge them, or say, 'We will never have them in our church!' We must be filled with compassion and see them as valuable and precious. If you see a man lying in the street, flat on his back and drunk, you need to see him as so valuable and precious that Jesus died for him on the cross. For God so loved the world – not only the Christians, the world – that He gave His only begotten Son. God loves every human being on the face of the earth. He might hate what they are doing at the time, but He loves every human being. He hates sin, but He loves people.

> But when he saw the multitudes, he was moved with compassion on them, because they fainted, and were scattered abroad, as sheep having no shepherd. Then saith he unto his disciples, 'The harvest truly is plenteous, but the labourers are few; Pray ye therefore the Lord of the harvest, that he will send forth labourers into his harvest' (Matt. 9.36–38).

If the harvest was plenteous 1900 years ago, how plenteous is it right now? Just think about that. Jesus told his disciples (and we are His disciples today, are we not?) to *pray the Lord of the harvest to send forth labourers into his harvest*. He did not say pray to God to save everybody, He said you must pray to God to send labourers. If you pray in

Jesus' name that God should send forth a labourer to the unsaved loved one, God will send forth a Wordstrong, Holy Spirit labourer across that person's path, and you will find that person coming to you and telling you that everybody he or she bumps into is talking to him or her about Jesus. You pray to God to send forth labourers and then you must be sensitive to the Holy Spirit, where He wants to guide and lead you to be a labourer to someone else.

You see, God is not confused, He knows that your family will not always listen to you: a prophet is not honoured in his own land or town or house. I had a hard time trying to get my own brothers saved, because I am younger and they, being older, thought, 'What does he know, anyway?' There is a lot of pride involved in family circles, but, if somebody whom they have known for years comes and talks to them, they might start listening to him, rather than you. God knows what He is doing. Say, for instance, that your son goes to karate lessons and his instructor, whom he respects a great deal, is born again and starts witnessing to your son about Jesus. Well, your son might think, if it can happen to that guy, it can happen to me as well. You see, sometimes our children do not identify with what happens to their parents, but they will identify with what happens to their friends.

> Be patient therefore, brethren, unto the coming of the Lord. Behold, the husbandman waiteth for the precious fruit of the earth, and hath long patience for it, until he receive the early and latter rain (Jas. 5.7).

The former and latter rain, in the natural world, referred to the rain that fell on the earth after the sowing, so that the seeds could germinate, and the rain that fell before the harvesting, just when the fruit was starting to appear, so that the fruit could get enough water and food to develop into good fruit and not dry up on the branches. This is the kind of rain we need in our spiritual lives as well: rain after the seeds are sown, and rain to make the fruit develop. In the spiritual world this means we must be ready to receive the Holy Spirit.

God is waiting for us to get into a position such that He can send the former and the latter rain combined. The former rain was in the Old Testament – the anointing that rested on a few selected prophets and kings; but we are to receive both the former and latter rain, together.

I believe that the character of God does not line up with a precious few folk, a minority, going to heaven, but that it is His desire to have an outpouring of the Holy Spirit in every nation until the minority will become the majority. People from every walk of life will be touched. I believe that the move of the Spirit of God has already started across the face of the earth – God is starting to move everywhere where people are getting in line with the Word of God and making themselves available for the Holy Spirit to work through them. God does not just want you to be able to do something, He will make you able; all you have to do is to be available.

8

Are you having Job's experience?

Many Christians have been taught that what happened to Job will automatically happen to them, that some time in their lives they will have a Job experience. So everybody was always saying that they were having a Job experience, but they never had the end results that Job had.

Firstly, I want you to know that, with Job, the experience only lasted nine months – so, if you are supposed to be having a Job experience, it should not drag on for ever: you should get through it and triumph in the end.

Secondly, if it was God who put the sickness on Job, if it was God who forced Job into the predicament, then, automatically, we should believe God for a similar experience. I want to do the will of God in every area of my life, I want to experience the blessings of God in every area of my life; I will do whatever He tells me to do, because I love Him and because I have committed my life to His service and a commandment has no choice involved in it. You either do it in obedience to what God desires you to do, or you do not and then you are being disobedient.

> There was a man in the land of Uz, whose name was Job; and that man was perfect and upright, and one that feared God, and eschewed evil (Job 1.1).

Those were his good points: he feared God and he

eschewed evil; the word 'perfect' means someone who is upright, with a sincere heart towards God: Job did not go around doing evil or committing sin.

> And it was so, when the days of their feasting were gone about, that Job sent and sanctified them, and rose up early in the morning, and offered burnt offerings according to the number of them all: for Job said it may be that my sons have sinned, and cursed God in their hearts. Thus did Job continually (Job 1.5).

That was done in absolute fear. He became anxious and prayed about it continually, instead of casting it upon God and leaving it to Him, living with faith in God's Word and in the covenant that we have with Him. You see, when you come into the kingdom of God, you become a covenant partner with God. We are going to see at the end of the book of Job, that when he did come and partake of the covenant that he had with God, God even forgave his friends through what Job did.

Why did Job have this fear that his children might have cursed God? Did he perhaps not do his fatherly duty, did he neglect to bring them up in reverence of God? Were they like Eli's children, Hophni and Phineas, whose father was upright before the Lord as well, but 'The sons of Eli were base and worthless; they did not know or regard the Lord' (1 Sam. 2.12, Amplified Bible). Does the word of God not teach us to 'Train up a child in the way he should go: and when he is old, he will not depart from it' (Prov. 22.6)? That is a spiritual law and was as true in the time of Job as it is today. Train up your child in the way he should go; do your duty towards your child, and trust in God to do the rest in his life: he shall not depart from the way he should go. If you have done your duty, you should not have any fear, you should trust in the Lord. Why did Job have this continual fear?

> For the thing which I greatly feared is come upon me, and that

> which I was afraid of is come unto me (Job 3.25).

There are some scriptures in the book of Proverbs concerning fear, for instance 'Be not afraid of sudden fear ....For the Lord shall be thy confidence, and shall keep thy foot from being taken' (Prov. 3.25–26). Now, fear of God, the respectful reverence that is due to Him, that is one thing, but Job was living in absolute fear. If you say: 'Oh, I do not know what I am going to do, I think maybe my sons and daughters are going to backslide; maybe I'd better pray for them tonight; maybe they are not right with God, maybe they are cursing God.' If you think and say this continually, you are not living by faith. Yet, this is what happens to some of us on a daily basis: some people have fretted about their children so much, that their children are praying for their parents now, because of the fretting.

> Then Satan answered the Lord, and said, Doth Job fear God for nought? Hast not thou made an hedge about him, and about his house, and about all that he has on every side? thou hast blessed the work of his hands, and his substance is increased in the land. But put forth thy hand now, and touch all that he hath, and he will curse thee to thy face (Job 1.9–11).

People read that and then they decide that God had put a hedge around Job, but when Satan came, God took the hedge down and that put Satan in a position to attack Job. First they say God allowed it, and then they decide it was God's will for Job to suffer; some go even further and actually say God was the one who brought the disaster on to Job. That is simply not true. The hedge was put up by God; He is not going to tear it down for no reason except to see Job suffering. *It makes no sense*. Why would He send His Son to redeem us from the hand of the enemy (Ps. 136.24), and then break our protection down and tell Satan to get us?

> And the Lord said unto Satan, Behold all that he hath is in thy power (Job 1.12).

Why does God make that statement? Well, Job was living in fear, as we saw.

> The fear of a man bringeth a snare: but whoso putteth his trust in the Lord shall be safe (Prov. 29.25).

> He that diggeth a pit shall fall into it, and *whoso breaketh an hedge, a serpent shall bite him* (Eccles. 10.8, italics mine).

Did Job not break his own hedge down, through his fear? Some people think that the more they go on at God, the more they cry out in an absolute fearful manner, the more it will cause God to move. God does not operate in that way. Jesus said that being anxious is not going to make you any taller, it is not going to help you one little bit. As a matter of fact, when you are in trouble, you should not get anxious, but allow faith and patience to operate so that you might receive God's promises. Being anxious is not going to move God at all. God has already moved, by sending His Son, before you were born. When you get into a walk of faith with God, you get yourself into a position to receive what He has already done for you.

Salvation did not come into being just when you got saved; it was here long before that, but, when you put yourself into a position to receive Jesus by faith, that which God had done already became a part of your life. That is why you cannot buy healing. Some people think if they do this or that, God will move to heal them. God has given His instructions in His Book; He has given us the Holy Spirit so we can be led by Him and God provided healing before you were born. You must get yourself into a position of forgiveness and love and faith to receive what God has already done for you.

We often find ourselves in a position like Job because we do not know the rules. Rule 1 is that I must know:
(a) who my enemy is;
(b) who my Father, my Protector, is; and

(c) who I am in Christ.

Some people blame God for everything that happens on the earth, and, according to them, the only thing the devil is responsible for is stealing people from their church. We go through a lot of unnecessary suffering because of tradition and religion. Job had three 'good' friends. Praise the Lord for Job in the end, otherwise I do not know what would have happened to them. I know plenty of friends like that.

When I got back from Bible school in America, the first thing some of the ministers in Johannesburg told me was that I would have to get a job to support myself; that it is extremely hard to be a minister in Johannesburg because of all the evil things that are happening in the city, and that it is almost impossible to get over 200 people for a service. Then they drank a little wine and told me: 'Thus saith the Lord.' I thought: 'No, that is not the Lord, that is the wine.'

Today, praise God, Rhema Ministries have thousands of born again believers in their Johannesburg congregation; there are branches right through Southern Africa and Britain and we do a lot of outreach work and video ministering in other countries. Do not listen to all the negative advice that friends give you – ask the Lord to reveal His will for your life to you and get in line with that. Be positive.

> Then Job arose, and rent his mantle, and shaved his head, and fell upon the ground, and worshipped, And said, Naked came I out of my mother's womb, and naked shall I return thither: the Lord gave and the Lord hath taken away; blessed be the name of the Lord (Job 1.20–21).

We have often heard that one used: 'The Lord gave and the Lord hath taken away.' You see, if the Lord gives and the Lord takes away, then what is the devil doing? Nothing, for he is neither giving, nor taking, he is doing nothing. The Bible will always show us how somebody acted or what they said under certain circumstances; in other words it records the facts, the events and statements made by people; and, although it will be a true statement of their behaviour, it does not necessarily mean that what they *said* was a statement of truth.

We must also understand that Job did not know what was happening in the spiritual realm; he did not see what was happening between God and Satan. *We* know because it is recorded for us in the first couple of chapters of the book. Therefore Job spoke things he did not understand (Job 42.3). He also did not have the full revelation of the character of God, which we have in the New Testament, so he thought of God as a terrible God, who is out to get you. Sure, he eschewed evil and did not sin, but he did it out of fear, not from a heart full of love for God. Because of this, Job said things about God that were not true. That is why it is so important to know the character of God, so that you know He loves you more than your earthly father ever can and you can trust in Him.

Jesus said in John 10:10 that the devil comes to steal, kill and destroy, but that He has come to give us life more abundantly. It must have been the devil who was doing the stealing, killing and destroying in Job's case, and God was the one in the end who blessed Job twice as much. God will test you, God will prove you, but not with evil. He does not have any evil to prove you with: God is a good God. If it is God's will for you to do something, then you had better submit and do it. It is terribly hard to go to somebody and, when you ask them if they believe that God wants them to be healed, they say, 'No, but pray for me.' Somebody actually said to me once: 'I believe that God put this sickness on me, but pray for me, anyhow.' I replied that I did not want to go against God's will. If He had put the sickness on the man and it was God's will for him to have it, then he had better keep it.

A lot of people asked me in the past: 'If you preach that God wants to heal, what happens to the ones who do not get healed?' Well, if I said that I do not know if God wants to heal or not, the first thing the devil would do is convince people that they are not the ones whom God wants to heal. Hope comes when you tell people that God wants to do something for them, not when you tell them that God wants to make them sick – if you have no hope, you have no faith, and how are you going to live then?

'The just shall live by his faith' (Habakkuk 2.4). When you start getting hope and putting your faith to it, you start believing God and you get encouraged by it; then you will see some wonderful things happening around you.

> Let no man say when he is tempted, I am tempted of God: for God cannot be tempted with evil, neither tempteth he any man (Jas. 1.13).

Now, you can say to me, is sickness evil? Well, let me ask you this question: was sickness on the earth before sin came? We should always go back to the garden of Eden, and see what God's ideas, place and will for man were. All the things that came on earth when Adam sinned must be related to sin. I am not saying if you are sick you are walking in sin, but if sickness was God's idea and God's will for man, then it should have been here before sin hit the earth; it should have been here before Satan came on to the scene. I mean, surely God does not have to rely on Satan to bring His will to pass. That is why I can tell you that prosperity is God's idea and God's will, because poverty came with Satan; and the reason why Satan will fight with the weapon of poverty, is because you cannot spread the gospel without being financially blessed by God.

> But every man is tempted, when he is drawn away of his own lust, and enticed. Then when lust hath conceived, it bringeth forth sin: and sin, when it is finished, bringeth forth death. Do not err, my beloved brethren. Every good gift and every perfect gift is from above, and cometh down from the Father of lights, with whom is no variableness, neither shadow of turning (Jas. 1.14–17).

In the light of the above, let us look at Job again, and at his friends:

> For the arrows of the Almighty are within me, the poison whereof drinketh up my spirit: the terrors of God do set themselves in array against me (Job. 6.4).

God did not set terror against him – that should be obvious from James 1.13. We saw in Job 1 that God said the hedge was already down, but that was because of Job's fear. People with a family history of sickness and disease will sometimes walk in so much fear of it that it will come on them – because most sicknesses are caused by fear, in any case. When it happens to them, they usually say: 'I always knew that I would get it, I knew it was going to happen.'

> I have sinned; what shall I do unto thee, O thou preserver of men? why hast thou set me as a mark against thee, so that I am a burden to myself (Job 7.20).

> For he breaketh me with a tempest, and multiplieth my wounds without cause. He will not suffer me to take my breath, but filleth me with bitterness (Job 9.17–18).

'Though he slay me, yet will I trust in him' (Job 13.15). God does not want to slay you and me; if He wanted to, He would have done it long ago. He is not out to slay you, but to save you, so that you can get somebody else into the kingdom of God.

> For it increaseth. Thou huntest me as a fierce lion: and again thou shewest thyself marvellous upon me (Job 10.16).

It is obvious that Job, as he himself confessed later, 'Uttered that I understood not; things too wonderful for me, which I knew not' (Job 42.3). Verse 6 says: 'Wherefore I abhor myself, and repent in dust and ashes.'

> I pray not that thou shouldest take them out of the world, but that thou shouldest keep them from evil (John 17.15).

Jesus prayed that God would not take you out of the world. Do you believe that God listened to Jesus' prayers? Not to be taken out of this world – not to be taken somewhere else, not to be slain.

> He teareth me in his wrath, who hateth me: he gnasheth upon me with his teeth; mine enemy sharpeneth his eyes upon me (Job 16.9).

> He hath made me also a byword of the people; and aforetime I was as a tabret (Job 17.6).

> Behold, I cry out of wrong, but I am not heard: I cry aloud, but there is no judgment. He hath fenced up my way that I cannot pass, and he hath set darkness in my paths (Job 19.7–8).

We can see here that Job's problem was not God; Job's problem was his lack of knowledge that made him a prey for the devil. The quicker Job could get his head up again and get into a position where he could receive what God desired him to have, stand on his covenant and resist the devil, the quicker the devil would flee from him and then God could bless him again.

Fear and lack of knowledge – that is our major problem. If you have knowledge in your heart, not head knowledge, you will be able to face every situation as it arises. James 1 says if you lack wisdom, ask God; if you do not have the wisdom to handle the situation, ask God who giveth to all men liberally, but ask in faith.

Jesus said that out of the abundance of the heart the mouth speaks – you can tell and locate a person by his speech. Faith will cause your speech to be in line with God's Word, but fear, which is perverted faith, causes you to speak in line with the devil's lies.

> Teach me, and I will hold my tongue: and cause me to understand wherein I have erred. How forcible are right words! (Job 6.24–25).

Now, that sounds good, but look at what he says after that:

> Therefore I will not refrain my mouth; I will speak in the anguish of my spirit; I will complain in the bitterness of my soul (Job 7.11).

That does not sound like speaking in faith to me! Neither does this:

> Though I am innocent and in the right, my own mouth would condemn me; though I am blameless, He would prove me perverse (Job 9.20, Amplified Bible).

When Job gets into a position of faith instead of fear, he gets his covenant working for him again, and look what happens:

> Then Job answered the Lord, and said, I know that thou canst do every thing, and that no thought can be withholden from thee. Who is he that hideth counsel without knowledge? therefore have I uttered that I understood not; things too wonderful for me, which I knew not. Hear, I beseech thee, and I will speak: I will demand of thee, and declare thou unto me. I have heard of thee by the hearing of the ear: but now mine eye seeth thee. Wherefore I abhor myself, and repent in dust and ashes.
>
> And it was so, that after the Lord hath spoken these words unto Job, the Lord said to Eliphaz the Temanite, My wrath is kindled against thee, and against thy two friends: for ye have not spoken of me the thing that is right, as my servant Job hath. Therefore take unto you now seven bullocks and seven rams, and go to my servant Job, and offer up for yourselves a burnt offering and my servant Job shall pray for you: for him I will accept (Job 42.1–8).

Why will Job be accepted? Because he got back under

that covenant and he is now operating under it and in faith.

> And the Lord turned the captivity of Job, when he prayed for his friends: also the Lord gave Job twice as much as he had before.... So the Lord blessed the latter end of Job more than his beginning: for he had fourteen thousand sheep, and six thousand camels, and a thousand yoke of oxen and a thousand she asses. He had also seven sons and three daughters.... After this lived Job an hundred and forty years, and saw his sons, and his sons' sons, even four generations. So Job died, being old and full of days (Job 42.10–17).

You see, some people never get out of the Job experience – thank God, Job did. I do not care what you are going through, come out of it like Job did. He got back more than he started off with.

There is something else that we can learn from verse 10 of chapter 42 – Job had to forgive his friends and pray for them; he must have been quite upset with them because of all the things they said to him, but verse 10 says: 'And the Lord turned the captivity of Job' – when? *when he prayed for his friends.* If you have anything against somebody that you cannot forgive them, the Lord cannot bless you the way that He wishes to do. Do not carry grudges, forgive them, pray for them, and you will be blessed.

I have seen the devil steal from the Body of Christ over the years, from people who love Jesus and long to establish His kingdom on this earth. But do not get discouraged: stand on your covenant with God, praise Him with your lips continually, walk in love and minister salvation to every human being you come into contact with. I believe God is going to restore sevenfold to you that which was stolen. Do not get bitter and twisted with God, come towards Him, do not run from Him – that is what Job did in the end – he came towards God. He was delivered out of the experience because he got into a position where God could bless him again.

9
Wisdom – pertinent truth

God's wisdom will give us insight into the true nature of things. If we have the wisdom of God operating in our lives and we listen to it and to the things of God, it will totally change our lives. To find out in depth about wisdom, we are going to study the book of Proverbs.

All wisdom comes from God. The New Testament talks about man's wisdom and God's wisdom, but I found out that if you are not operating in God's wisdom, then you are not operating in wisdom at all. Man's wisdom is no wisdom at all; without God's wisdom it is foolishness.

God established certain spiritual principles on the earth and you can either make them work for you or against you – working *with* these principles is wise, working against them, foolish.

> But where shall wisdom be found? and where is the place of understanding? Man knoweth not the price thereof; neither is it found in the land of the living. The depth saith, It is not in me: and the sea saith, It is not with me. It cannot be gotten for gold, neither shall silver be weighed for the price thereof. It cannot be valued with the gold of Ophir, with the precious onyx, or the sapphire. The gold and the crystal cannot equal it: and the exchange of it shall not be for jewels of fine gold. No mention shall be made of coral, or of pearls: for the price of wisdom is above rubies. The topaz of Ethiopia shall not equal it, neither

> shall it be valued with pure gold. Whence then cometh wisdom? and where is the place of understanding? Seeing it is hid from the eyes of all living, and kept close from the fowls of the air. Destruction and death say, We have heard the fame thereof with our ears. God understandeth the way thereof, and he knoweth the place thereof. For he looketh to the ends of the earth, and seeth under the whole heaven; To make the weight for the winds; and he weigheth the waters by measure. When he made a decree for the rain, and a way for the lightning of the thunder: Then did he see it, and declare it; he prepared it, yea, and searched it out. And unto man he said, Behold, the fear of the Lord, that is wisdom; and to depart from evil is understanding (Job 28.12–28).

> The fear of the Lord is the beginning of wisdom: a good understanding have all they that do his commandments (Ps. 111.10).

> The fear of the Lord is the beginning of knowledge: but fools despise wisdom and instruction (Prov. 1.7).

All wisdom begins when you get into a position where you have the knowledge that God is God: when you have reverence for Him and respect for the Word of God and God Himself. His Word is wisdom.

Jesus is God's Word in the flesh, therefore Jesus is wisdom. You should have reverence and respect for what Jesus said and who Jesus is. Some people say: 'How can you be so dumb as to believe in God, to believe in Jesus?' But when you ask them what they believe, and where they think we came from, they say they believe we came from swampgas; then we developed into a fish, they say, then we looked like the fowls of the air, finally our wings fell off, and there you are. I want to tell you that that is more dumb than anything that I believe in. It is not dumb to believe in God: it is the beginning of all wisdom.

To have reverence for God's Word is wisdom: to study it is to increase your wisdom. I want you to commit yourself to study one chapter of the book of Proverbs every day for a month. It will take you a month to get through it, so you can read chapter one on the first, chapter two on the second, and so on. I believe if you do that it will change your life and provide you with a practical way to organise and live your life. Many people who are Christians become so heavenly minded that they are no earthly good: they are no good to their bosses, their wives or husbands, their children or to people around them. They are walking around as super-spiritual beings, pretending to be something that they are not, and that does not lead to being a good witness for Christianity.

> My son, if thou wilt receive my words, and hide my commandments with thee; So that thou incline thine ear unto wisdom, and apply thine heart to understanding; Yea, if thou criest after knowledge, and liftest up thy voice for understanding; If thou seekest her as silver, and searchest for her as for hid treasures; Then thou shall understand the fear of the Lord, and find the knowledge of God. For the Lord giveth wisdom: out of his mouth cometh knowledge and understanding (Prov. 2.1–6).

What is God's mouthpiece today? The Word of God; and Jesus was the Word walking around in the flesh. In the beginning was the Word, and the Word was with God, and the Word was God.

> He layeth up sound wisdom for the righteous: he is a buckler to them that walk uprightly (Prov. 2.7).

Wisdom and knowledge are two separate things. This is how it works: firstly, you get knowledge from the Word of God. As you read it, you increase your knowledge, your understanding of the facts. Then you need God to give you understanding to arrange the facts, and then wisdom to allow you to apply the facts. A lot of people have a good knowledge of God's Word, yet they never get to a point where they walk in victory because they do not have the wisdom of God to apply that knowledge. You may be able to quote every scripture on healing in the Bible, but still be sick if you do not adapt to the wisdom of God and begin to apply it.

The way to allow the Word of God to operate is to meditate on God's Word. If you can get it into your spirit, you must then ask for God's wisdom to enable you to apply it to your circumstances and change them.

Two people can finish Bible school at the same time, and the one will go out and cause more confusion and problems in the Body of Christ than anyone else and the other one will go out and make a success of whatever he is doing. Both of them learned the same things, had the same teachers, saw the same videos and sat in the same classes the same length of time. One might have a great knowledge of the Word, but if you lack the ability to apply it, you lack wisdom.

1 Corinthians 1.30 tells us that Jesus is made unto us wisdom. When you are born again, you have the ability of the mind of Christ – you get the wisdom of God – but it is the same ability that a little baby gets when he or she is born. When you were six months old you had the same muscles, hands, feet, hips, eyes and jaw that you have now – you did not get new ones when you grew older, or receive another eye when you reached the age of ten; you just grew up physically and you developed the abilities that you were given when you were born.

We need to develop our spirits in the same way: we have the attributes of God, the mind of Christ, Jesus has been made unto us wisdom, but we are going to have to exercise, we are going to have to eat spiritual food. The breakfast of the Christians is not Kellogg's Corn Flakes, the breakfast of the champions is God's Word.

Some people have been saved for ten years or longer, but they still look like babies, spiritually. Oh, if we could only get to the place where we operate in the wisdom of God, everything we do, yes, everything we put our hand to will prosper. As Pastor Reinhard Bonnke says: 'Everything that God orders, He pays for.'

Now, Proverbs 4 explains to us how to walk in the wisdom of God.

> Let thine heart retain my words: keep my commandments, and live. Get wisdom, get understanding: forget it not; neither decline from the words of my mouth. Forsake her not, and she shall preserve thee: love her, and she shall keep thee (Prov. 4.4–6).

Jesus said if you love Him, you will keep His commandments; so if you do not keep Jesus' commandments, you do not love him.

> Wisdom is the principal thing; therefore get wisdom: and with all thy getting get understanding. Exalt her, and she shall promote thee: she shall bring thee to honour, when thou dost embrace her. She shall give to thine head an ornament of grace: a crown of glory shall she deliver to thee. Hear, O my son, and receive my sayings; and the years of thy life shall be many (Prov. 4.7–10).

When you study the book of Proverbs, you will find that David taught everything that he knew to Solomon; the Hebrew custom was like that: the father would pass all his knowledge on to his son. The minute that they stopped doing that, the son would turn his back on God and become reprobate. If you will discipline your life in front of your children, be an example to them, and train them up, they will grow up to be men and women of God.

> And Solomon loved the Lord, walking in the statutes of David his father: only he sacrificed and burnt incense in high places. And the king went to Gibeon to sacrifice there; for that was the great high place: a thousand burnt offerings did Solomon offer upon that altar. In Gibeon the Lord appeared to Solomon in a

> dream by night: and God said, Ask what I shall give thee (1 Kgs. 3.3–5).

Can you imagine the Lord coming to you today and saying: 'Ask what you want, I am El Shaddai, ask what you want and I will give it to you.' What would you ask for? A new swimming pool? A new motor-car?

Some people have heard just enough of prosperity to become interested, and all that they want to hear, is what *they* want to hear. When I start counselling and straightening them out, they leave the church. If you think that God is going to prosper you and bless your business and give you a ministry while you are committing adultery and while you are stealing money from the business and not paying the people who work for you their salaries, forget it. A lot of people on the outside will say: 'Oh, we do not understand it; that brother gives, he confesses the Word, he is a faith man.' *No!* I'll tell you what he is: he is a deceived man!

> And Solomon said, Thou hast shewed unto thy servant David my father great mercy, according as he walked before thee in truth, and in righteousness, and in uprightness of heart with thee; and thou hast kept for him this great kindness, that thou hast given him a son to sit on his throne, as it is this day. And now, O LORD my God, thou hast made thy servant king instead of David my father: and I am but a little child: I know not how to go out or come in. And thy servant is in the midst of thy people which thou hast chosen, a great people, that cannot be numbered nor counted for multitude (1 Kgs. 3.6–8).

Solomon is saying to God that his first concern is for God's people. He wanted the wisdom of God to handle the people, to be able to rule over them according to God's will. Verse 9 does not say: 'Give therefore thy servant four swimming pools, twelve pairs of shoes and fifteen suits,' it says: 'Give therefore thy servant an understanding heart to judge thy people, that I may discern between good and bad: for who is able to judge this thy so great a people?'

Solomon chose wisdom and understanding to judge Israel in true justice; he desired gifts that would best qualify him for his calling in life. Too often people pray for gifts which, they think, will make them look great in the eyes of others, and they might not be called to do that particular kind of work. You see, God has got enough of everything to give everybody what they ask, but He looks into your heart to see the reason why you ask a particular gift.

God is not saying, well, if brother Smith buys an extra suit, we are not going to have enough to feed so and so. He will make the righteous prosper to spread the gospel; the Bible says that the riches of the unjust are laid up for the righteous. I believe that some of us will be able to walk into a place and buy things for a twentieth of the price it normally costs, because we will have the wisdom of God to get it; but if our motive to get the wisdom of God is to buy things, we are not going to get it.

Let me give you an example. One day, not so long ago, the people in my church took up an offering for me and my wife personally. When I came on to the platform to receive it, I asked the Lord why He was doing it, because I knew that it was the Spirit of God who was doing it. The Lord said to me that there were people in the gathering that morning without money or food or transport and He wanted me to feed them all and give them money for petrol. So, when all that money came to the front, for me to receive it, I said: 'Thank you, Lord, I will be your channel.' Then I called for people who were experiencing a lack to come and see me in the back of the church – and I had the time of my life. It is a great feeling to take a bucket full of money and have people around you and just to hand it out to people who you know do not have enough, just to be a blessing to them. When the bucket was empty and the people's needs were met, a man came up to me and gave me three times the amount I had in the bucket in the first place: that is being blessed coming in and going out. But do not be deceived, if you are going to take a bucket of money and hand it out to people because you want the Lord to multiply it back to you: if that is your reason for doing it, instead of compassion for the people and the desire to help them, then you are missing the whole point.

Solomon's choice fitted in with his calling in life. If you are a businessman, I would advise you to spend more time with the Lord in the mornings, instead of trying to make a living, rushing around from one place to the next. Then you will be able to walk into a place and God will give you the wisdom to do a transaction in thirty seconds that would normally have taken you thirty days. Moreover, it will be a better deal, for without God on your side it would have been the wrong deal in any case, and it would have backfired on you.

You have the wisdom of God in you; you must exercise it and develop it. I know a preacher who went before God and said: 'Father, I am so busy that I do not have enough time to spend in prayer before You; what shall I do?' And the Lord said to him: 'Give me more time.' The man did that and he says whereas he never used to have more than half an hour to spend with the Lord, he started to give God an hour every day and he found out that by giving God more of his time, he had the wisdom of God operating in his life and he did everything else in half the time that he used to do it in before.

That is why I leave a lot of the counselling in my church to other anointed men, so that I can spend more time before God praying and listening to God. It would be useless for me to try and counsel everybody in as large a congregation as we have and neglect seeking God's wisdom. I have to discipline myself to get into the Word at least three to four hours a day and to get before God and get sensitive to God, so that I will know what God's will for my church is.

And the speech pleased the Lord, that Solomon had asked this thing (1 Kgs. 3.10).

Solomon had his priorities right. I asked the Lord a little while ago why we get 350 people saved during a healing campaign and the next week we can only find three or four of them. The Lord told me that most of those people come to God as a last resort, like a lucky dip packet, to try and get healed and they think that by coming up for the altar call to get saved, they will get God to move in their lives. They do not really want to get born again, they are just coming forward, because they think if they do, God will heal them. A lot of people will try everything else first and, at last, when there is nothing else left they will try God, but only as a last resort. Now I am not saying that God does not want to heal you, He does. But you must get your priorities right: do not come before God with ulterior motives in your heart. If you come to be born again, you should have a desire in your heart to be born again and to serve God. Do not come to be born again because actually you do not want to, but you need God's healing power in your life. Remember, you can lie to men, but you cannot lie to God: He sees into your heart. What happens with these people is that they pray the prayer of salvation but they do not believe it in their hearts, and as they are leaving they think: 'Well, I've prayed that prayer, I came to church and nothing is happening so I cannot believe that healing and salvation actually work.' So they leave and we do not see them again, no matter how many times we try to contact them again.

Now, healing, salvation and prosperity work, otherwise Jesus died for no reason on that cross; and you should give when you have a need, that is a spiritual law. But if your motive in giving is solely to get, forget it: it does not please God.

> And God said unto him, Because thou hast asked this thing, and hast not asked for thyself long life; neither has asked riches for thyself, nor has asked the life of thine enemies; but has asked for

> thyself understanding to discern judgment; Behold, I have done according to thy words: lo, I have given thee a wise and understanding heart; so that there was none like thee before thee, neither after thee shall any arise like unto thee. And I have also given thee that which thou hast not asked, both riches, and honour: so that there shall not be any among the kings like unto thee all thy days (1 Kgs. 3.11–13).

God did not say in verse 13: 'And I have taken everything away from you, so that you might be humble and holy, for I hate riches....' God is the originator of prosperity, it is His idea that we may prosper, that we should be blessed coming in and going out. It is His idea that when we make a deal, we will be the ones to prosper more than anybody else. It is His idea that we have the wisdom of God so that whatever we put our hand to will prosper. It is His idea, and He is not concerned about it if you drive an expensive car, He wants you to have the best, but...but – *He wants you to have Him first in your life and not the car or the riches, the possessions. Put God first in your life.*

> Seek ye first the kingdom of God, and his righteousness; and all these things shall be added unto you (Matt. 6.33).

That is where a lot of people go wrong: they are trying to prosper without seeking Him first. They might, for instance, hear the testimony of John Osteen: how his wife, Jody, was diagnosed to go home and die with cancer, yet she is healed today. Some people, however, do not hear the rest of the story, how they walked up and down their home, confessing the Word day and night, night and day. Up and down, up and down; and they stood on the Word, they took hold of it and claimed that healing and fought the good fight of faith until that cancer left her.

You see, you are in a fight with the devil, and he will bring things against you, but, thank God, the fight is not over until you have won. Do not give up halfway – we are more than conquerors through Christ, He has won the fight for us already, we just have to claim the victory. He said that we can overcome the world and the devil is the prince or ruler of this world, so we can overcome him, through Christ Jesus. We can do all things through Him. Hallelujah!

A woman came to one of our meetings once, while Kenneth Hagin was here and she brought with her a man who was dying. She said the man only had twenty-four hours to live and she wanted Kenneth Hagin to pray for him. When I told her that, unfortunately, Brother Hagin would not be there until that evening (which meant she had to wait a couple of hours), she said that she could not wait, because she had other things to do. Now, I ask you, if the man was so sick that he was going to die in twenty-four hours, what was so important that she could not sit down and wait for a few hours and get the man healed? She would not wait, she took the man home to die. That is not the way the wisdom of God works.

When Jesus multiplied the fish, they put Him on their shoulders and they said: 'Let us make Him king, Hosannah!' But when they took Him to the cross, those guys who carried Him on their shoulders were gone. When He started to work miracles, everybody wanted to put Him on their shoulders; when they condemned Him to death and took Him to the cross on Calvary, everybody started spitting on Him. One day, while I was still in Bible school in America, the Spirit of the Lord came on me and I began to cry and the Lord said to me: 'Son, from this day you will know for eternity that you follow Me, not because of the fish, but because of who I am.' So, do not follow Him because of the fish, not because of the miracles or the things that you can have, but because of who He is.

You know, if that rich young man gave up everything he had and followed Jesus, he would have been the wealthiest man in all the tribes of Israel; because Jesus said that He was going to give him a hundredfold. One hundredfold of what he already had; but he loved money more than he loved Jesus, so he got nothing. We need wisdom in our lives.

> And God gave Solomon wisdom and understanding exceeding much, and largeness of heart, even as the sand that is on the sea shore. And Solomon's wisdom excelled the wisdom of all the children of the east country, and all the wisdom of Egypt. For he was wiser than all men; than Ethan the Ezrahite, and Heman, and Chalcol, and Darda, the sons of Mahol: and his fame was in all nations round about. And he spake three thousand proverbs: and his songs were a thousand and five. And he spake of trees, from the cedar tree that is in Lebanon even unto the hyssop that springeth out of the wall: he spake also of beasts, and of fowl and of creeping things, and of fishes. And there came of all people to hear the wisdom of Solomon, from all kings of the earth which had heard of his wisdom (1 Kgs. 4.29–34).

We have the ability to walk in the wisdom of God.

> Happy is the man that findeth wisdom, and the man that getteth understanding. For the merchandise of it is better than the merchandise of silver, and the gain thereof than fine gold. She is more precious than rubies: and all the things thou canst desire are not to be compared unto her. Length of days is in her right hand; and in her left hand riches and honour. Her ways are ways of pleasantness, and all her paths are peace. She is a tree of life to them that lay hold upon her: and happy is every one that retaineth her (Prov. 3.13–18).

God dealt with me and said I am not to open my mouth, unless I mean it. He said: 'You are patting people on the back and saying things because you love people and you just want everybody to be happy. I did not tell you to do that, I said what you say out of your mouth, you had better back up and do; and if you cannot back it up, then tell the person straight to his face that you cannot do it.' I said: 'Yes, Sir. I am not going to open my mouth any more, unless I mean it.'

If you are sincere with God, the truth shall set you free so stick to the truth.

> That your faith should not stand in the wisdom of men, but in the power of God (1 Cor. 2.5).

All real wisdom comes from God; Paul is saying here that there is some so-called wisdom that is really not God's wisdom. It is the so-called wisdom of the world; do not put your faith in that, but in the power of God.

> Howbeit we speak wisdom among them that are perfect: yet not the wisdom of this world, nor of the princes of this world, that come to nought: But we speak the wisdom of God in a mystery, even the hidden wisdom, which God ordained before the world unto our glory (1 Cor. 2.6–7).

It is a mystery to the world that if someone says he hates you, you can say say, 'I love you.' They cannot believe it.

> Which none of the princes of this world knew: for had they known it, they would not have crucified the Lord of glory. But as it is written, Eye hath not seen, nor ear heard, neither have entered into the heart of man, the things which God hath prepared for them that love him. But God hath revealed them unto us by his Spirit: for the Spirit searcheth all things, yea, the deep things of God (1 Cor. 2.8–10).

Praise God, it does not stop after verse 9; we will not only find out one day in the sweet by and by, we can get understanding of God's things now, by revelation through the Holy Spirit.

> For what man knoweth the things of a man, save the spirit of man which is in him? even so the things of God knoweth no man, but the Spirit of God. Now we have received, not the spirit

> of the world, but the spirit which is of God; that we might know the things which are freely given to us of God. Which things also we speak, not in the words which man's wisdom teacheth, but the Holy Ghost teacheth; comparing spiritual things with spiritual (1 Cor. 2.11–13).

We teach the wisdom of God, through the Spirit of God, but we are going to have to develop it. We have to spend time in the Word of God and praying; spend time being sensitive to the Spirit of God.

> Who is a wise man and endued with knowledge among you? let him shew out of a good conversation his works with meekness of wisdom. But if you have bitter envying and strife in your hearts, glory not, and lie not against the truth (Jas. 3.13–14).

If you have strife in your life, then the wisdom of God is not operating in your life, and every time you do something that is against the Word of God, you are lying against the truth.

It is about time that we started hearing about the other side of the Bible; some of us read it like this: 'I am blessed with spiritual blessings – now, let me see: "Love one another as I..." No, that is not for me...Let me look for something else...Oh, yes..."I wish above all things that you may prosper and be in good health..." Yes, that is it... "but if you have any sin in your life, confess it..." No, wait, let me go back to Psalm 91.' If we are Word people, then let us be Word-Whole-People; let us be complete Word people, not just promise people, because if you become Complete-Word-People, the promises will come by themselves.

> This wisdom descendeth not from above, but is earthly, sensual, devilish. For where envying and strife is, there is confusion and every evil work. But the wisdom that is from above is first pure, then peaceable, gentle, and easy to be intreated, full of mercy and good fruits, without partiality, and without hypocrisy (Jas. 3.15–17).

I used to think that any wisdom that people in the world operate under is earthly, sensual and devilish, but there are people in the world who are not operating under the devilish wisdom, even though they are not saved. I have found some people in the world who are not born again, and who have more wisdom in running their business than Christians. At least they realise that if you only work for five hours a day, you are going to reap the rewards of someone who only works five hours a day, and if you work for eight hours or more every day, that is the kind of reward that is due to you. 'What you sow, you shall also reap' is a spiritual law and it operates both ways; it will work for the sinner who is not born again, as well as for you: it will work against you, as well as for you.

If you are called into the ministry, then go into the ministry. Do not use your boss's time, that he is paying you to do his work in, to start counselling people on the telephone. Give your boss what he pays you for: an honest day's work. Do your counselling during your lunch break or after hours. If God has called you to work in an office, then be the best worker in that office, and give God the glory for it. We should be an example to the world – that is the wisdom of God. The world should see it in us – the wisdom of God.

God is looking for people who can be vessels and channels that will represent Him in these last days; people who will not only walk in the faith that they have seen through His Word, not only walking in the prosperity that He has laid up for His children; but will walk in the full counsel of the holiness of His Word, for He did not come to condemn, but to set free. Hallelujah.

A Sinner's Prayer to Receive Jesus as Saviour

Dear Heavenly Father...

I come to you in the name of Jesus.

Your Word says '...him that cometh to me I will in no wise cast out' (John 6.37).

So I know you won't cast me out, but you take me in, and I thank you for it.

You said in your Word, 'Whosoever shall call upon the name of the Lord shall be saved' (Romans 10.13). I am calling on your name, so I know you have saved me now.

You also said, 'If thou shalt confess with thy mouth the Lord Jesus, and shalt believe in thine heart that God hath raised him from the dead, thou shalt be saved. For with the heart man believeth unto righteousness; and with the mouth confession is made unto salvation' (Romans 10.9–10).

I believe in my heart Jesus Christ is the Son of God. I believe that He was raised from the dead for my justification.

And I confess Him now as my Lord, because your Word says, '...with the heart man believeth unto righteousness...' and I do believe with my heart.

I have now become the righteousness of God in Christ (2 Corinthians 5.21)...And I am saved!

Thank you, Lord!

Miracle Power

by Jamie Buckingham

There are no limits to what God may choose to do to - and through - us.

'Miracles should be the norm in the life of the Christian', insists Jamie Buckingham. 'Because we are constantly stumbling through a dark world, we need God to guide our footsteps, giving us the ability to walk supernaturally.

'That means miracles. But God is not restoring miracles to the church. They've been there all along. He is simply waiting for simple people who will step forward in faith and expect God to use them.'

Jamie Buckingham has experienced many miracles himself in the course of his long ministry. His study of miracles in the New Testament and today - miracles of healing, power, provision and hope - is designed 'to stimulate you, excite you and hopefully to convince you that the miracles of Jesus were not for yesterday - they are for today.'

Jamie Buckingham is the author of many books including *Risky Living*, *Where Eagles Soar* and *The Truth Will Set You Free, But First It Will Make You Miserable*.

Kingsway Publications